Living 2 Die or Dying 2 Live

Barron K. Haywood MBA

outskirtspress
DENVER, COLORADO

The opinions expressed in this manuscript are solely the opinions of the author and do not represent the opinions or thoughts of the publisher. The author has represented and warranted full ownership and/or legal right to publish all the materials in this book.

Living 2 Die or Dying 2 Live
All Rights Reserved.
Copyright © 2013 Barron K. Haywood MBA
v2.0

Cover Photo © 2013 fotolia.com . All rights reserved - used with permission.

This book may not be reproduced, transmitted, or stored in whole or in part by any means, including graphic, electronic, or mechanical without the express written consent of the publisher except in the case of brief quotations embodied in critical articles and reviews.

Outskirts Press, Inc.
http://www.outskirtspress.com

ISBN: 978-1-4327-8980-0

Outskirts Press and the "OP" logo are trademarks belonging to Outskirts Press, Inc.

PRINTED IN THE UNITED STATES OF AMERICA

"For we don't live for ourselves our die for ourselves. If we live, it's to honor the Lord. And if we die, it's to honor the Lord. So whether we live or die, we belong to the Lord."
Romans 14; 7-8

"I dedicate this book to my daughters and family, through whom I have finally found LOVE, AMBITION, and the MOTIVATION to go on living."

Thank you GOD for bringing strong and positive people into my life, when I needed them to lean on for Strength, Hope, and Guidance through the ever changing roads of our existence. First and foremost, I praise and glorify God for allowing me to share my testimony with the world.

"I LOVE YOU GOD"

Author's Bio

A Born Again believer in GOD, Barron Keith Haywood has used GOD's simple principles to guide his life. A six-year Army Veteran. He is a graduate of St. Leo University and the University of Phoenix, with a BA in Accounting and a MBA in Business. Currently, Barron is the CEO of Black Baron Filmz. The author resides in Atlanta, GA.

Table of Contents

1	Blessing 2 the World	1
2	The Beginning	5
3	I'm Just Feeling Myself	17
4	Walk With Me LORD	20
5	Do The Right Thing	24
6	"Young Macaronii"	34
7	Growing Pains	41
8	Recruit 2 Army Soldier	49
9	Test of Faith	71
10	Finding GOD Again	83
11	Using God as a Guiding Light	102
12	Phoenix	105
13	Pray 4 ME	110
	To My Readers	117
	Contact Information:	119

1

Blessing 2 the World

Born on May 2, 1972, entering this world as a bastard and was given the name Barron by my Godmother, who also was my mother's nurse in the delivery room at Brackenridge Hospital. This may sound crazy but I still can remember the hospital as being cold and dark place with lighting just over the nursery area where all the new born babies were being placed. When emerging from my mother's womb, I was too stubborn to cry. The delivery doctor had to try all kinds of techniques to make me cry. Once, the delivery doctor was able to coax a wail from me I inhaled and came alive. GOD had chosen me on that day to remain in this world, and to become one of his faithful and fearful servants.

When kings are born, many are misunderstood as stubborn or hardheaded children. GOD giving me the gift of a king's mentality and characteristics, made life difficult for me initially because grownups did not understand my ways and did not recognize the destiny that GOD had chosen for me. Being labeled as a very stubborn child and not listening to any type of authority led to many meetings with leather belts and extension cords.

LIVING 2 DIE OR DYING 2 LIVE

Future kings rarely submit to anyone's authority and the child's baron spirit is hardly ever broken. Being born prematurely my birth size was so small that I could fit into large adult male hands. Believing those hands were GOD's. My doctor had given up hope on me but GOD did not and he comforted me, while fighting every day for my life to stay and live in this world. That fighting spirit stayed with me and was instantly noticed by my Godmother; as she looked into my baby brown eyes, those young eyes told her a story that this baby was going to be a future leader for mankind.

As a premature new born baby my only protection was provided by my Godmother's while sleeping in the all white nursery bed. My Godmother knew and prophesied, that "I would be a child who would rise above all obstacles and become a man of power, respect, and dignity". I only wish that my Godmother had lived long enough to see her prophesy become reality.

My mother, a beautiful dark skinned country girl, was as mean as a hornet's nest if anyone messed with her. When my mother graduated from high school, she and her parents moved from Bastrop to Austin, Texas, in search of a better life. My mother was only 19 years old at the time of my birth, and inherited the instant burden and responsibilities of raising her child alone, as many single parent mothers have to do today. There is a reason why GOD made women so strong in mind and spirit, because GOD knew this world would be unkind to most of them. Many single parent mother's take the best care of their children with a limited amount of resources.

My mother and her parents bought a small white house on 14th street in Austin. This is where most of my summer infant days were spent in the Texas hot summer heat sitting in my mother's lap rocking back and forth in an old faded wooden chair on the house porch. There were big pecan trees in the front yard that only provided so much shade during the day. The only real relief from the Texas heat you would get is when the sun started to fade and descend in the West.

My biological father would drop in from time to time, but he never made any attempt to become a permanent person in my life. As I grew into a young child I wish that I could have had a relationship with my father. Even though I did not grow up with love, I still yearned to love people and have them love me back.

Growing up during the 1970's was the result of why I love to see people working together and helping each other out. The 70's were great years for blacks; it was a time that blacks had a strong sense of unity within their community. They stuck together, and the music during this period reflected on the struggles, injustices, and oppression that blacks suffered at the hands of some whites in America.

There were more job opportunities for blacks in the inner city than in rural towns during the 1970's. Even though many blacks worked in the city they were sometimes still not allowed in upscale white stores. My mother told me stories about how my grandmother would take a shoestring to measure my mother's foot and with the shoestring marked; my grandmother would then present the shoestring to a white shoe store owner. The store owner would then walk to the back of the store where the shoes were housed and after several minutes would emerge from the back of the store with shoes that matched the size of the marked string. If the new shoe did not fit my mother's foot, the sale was final because a shoe tried on by a black customer could not be resold to a white customer. Yes, in southern states African-Americans were still not allowed in some shoe stores frequented by whites -- even after the passage of the 1964 Civil Rights Act.

LIVING 2 DIE OR DYING 2 LIVE

As the oldest girl in her family, my mother had to help raise her younger siblings. Her chores were cleaning the house, washing dishes, and clothes. My mother did not learn how to cook; she left that task to her younger sister Eddie Jean.

Mother had many stories to tell about her childhood in Bastrop, Texas, and about the people in her community. These stories were not about elaborate things, they were more about the simple things in life, like planting and working in a garden on their land. All of the vegetables that were cooked for family meals were fresh from the garden. If a cow was butchered the entire community would share the meat of the cow. There were always chickens in the yard, so if you wanted to eat chicken you had to catch one.

2

The Beginning

My mother met my stepfather when I was only three month's old; my biological father had moved to California and left us behind. My stepfather took on the responsibility of raising me, because he came from a good family and was a minister's son. My stepfather also served in the U.S. military during the Vietnam War.

The Vietnam War was tough on the American youth during this era because most Americans who served in the U.S. armed forces and are unfortunately deployed into combat, the soldiers that return home never return the way they left. There are many physical and emotional stressors that are derived from war and military service. Soldiers returning from war or any conflict find that the transition from military life to civilian life can be challenging. Many soldiers' are forgotten by society once they are discharged from military service. Many war veterans sacrifice their youth and life to keep the peace and freedom in the country that they serve. These countries then thank them by putting them on heavy medication to help suppress some of their incurable violent experiences, thoughts, and emotions.

LIVING 2 DIE OR DYING 2 LIVE

Many soldiers and veterans who do not receive proper treatment for service connected illnesses have a history of using illegal drugs to help relieve some of the trauma that they experienced while serving. Some veterans are sent to prison for their violent behavior and acts against society, but are they really at fault? Their violence is the result of intensive and combative training received during their call of duty, which some veterans cannot simply turn off. Stats have shown that even veterans who have non-combat tours still experience mental issues after being discharged from military service.

My stepfather grew up on the eastside of town in Austin, where most blacks lived. The eastside of town was like a big playground; everything was within walking distance -- the best food, shopping, churches and night clubs. The projects were the heart and soul of the eastside. It was also where you could find my step-father gathering and getting into mischief with his friends.

Back then, the projects were not a place where only drugs and violence existed; some projects were very functional and formed a good and viable community. Furthermore, the projects were a place where blacks lived temporarily until they could purchase their first home; only later did it become a permanent residence. The parents in the projects raised strong, intelligent, beautiful children. Some of the best athletes, leaders, scientists, songwriters, singers, actors, actresses and business moguls are just some of the success stories that the projects have produced around the world.

The first few years of my adolescent life I live in one of the projects in Austin, Texas. Meadow Brooks was where I spent most of my days shooting marbles under the only big oak tree surrounded by dirt near my apartment. I was the type of child that mostly played alone because it seemed that I was the

THE BEGINNING

youngest kid on the block. I never really bothered any one nor was I aspiring to be a menace, but my laid back demeanor was tested one day when I was playing outside on the steps in front of my apartment door.

A young boy from the neighborhood approach me while I was playing near the faded sidewalk and started to shake me down for all of my toys that I was playing with and everything that I had in my blue jean cut off short pockets. This was the first time that I remember using my physical strengthen against someone and it scared the hell out of me. Once I regained my conciseness of what I was doing to this would be jacker. I only remember someone pulling me off that boy that day while I continued to beat he is bloody skull against the concrete side walk where I was playing. Witnesses that saw the attempted shakedown told my mother that I was not at fault and the boy provoked me until I open a can of wipe ass on him. From that day forward I promised myself and was too scared to release the incredible hulk that had remained dormant inside of me. Once my anger reaches a certain level it continues to spiral out of control until it turns into a blackout rage. Consequences for my actions never brings me back to the reality of what I am about to do to the person who has just pushed my buttons.

My stepfather and mother dated for about two years, before my sister was born in June of 1974. After a few years passed and I reached the first grade, my parents decided to live together, and bought a home in Dove Springs -- a new subdivision on the Southside of Austin.

Dove Springs consisted of a great many service members, who were stationed or retired from Bergstrom Air Force base. I remember pulling up in the driveway of our new house and not seeing any grass in the yard, just dirt. Once we settled into our new home, my mom started a flower garden in the front of the house and a vegetable garden in the back. A small creek ran in the back of our house -- there was always water in it, but it never overflowed when there were heavy or prolonged rains. I spent a great deal of time in the creek playing with the small tadpoles and crawfish. I even tried to keep some of the crawfish as pets, but they always died after a couple of days in a pickle jar.

My mom, dad, sister and I planted fruit trees on the side of our house that always had sweet fruit on them, before the insects and birds got to them.

The hot rays from the summer sun left the drive way concrete warm while I laid on it as the sun started to set in the west. At night I would lay on the concrete with just a white tee shirt on behind my parent's parked cars in the driveway with my eyes focused on the many stars lighting up in the now black sky. There seemed to be a million little lights in the peaceful night sky, so when I would see some stars flash by, I immediately closed both of my eyes, while simultaneously make wishes on those falling stars. My street Tamarisk Circle really was peaceful at night and as well as the entire new neighborhood. While keeping my eyes closed for hours, I would sometimes fall asleep under the stars as they then watched over me in the two car driveway.

I loved my new residence, a small three-bedroom yellow and brown ranch house, but it seemed really big when I was little. My parents held their wedding reception there, as well as and small family parties.

My main source of entertainment in the house back then, when I was not able to play outside, because of rain or extreme heat, was a small brown piano that we had in the living room and a old record player that played LPs or 45s. I remember

THE BEGINNING

playing records like Michael Jackson, Rick James, Double Dutch bus, Prince, the TIME, OJAY's, and the GAP Band, and so on. I did not like being in the house for very long, though but passed my time with music.

Playing outside all day until the sun set and the streetlights started to glow was very normal for me. The streetlights were used as my external watch; when they came on, I knew that it was time for me to make my way home, because, the dark night sky was not far behind.

There were days when I had money I would ride my black huffy bike to the local 7-11 convenience store that was located a few blocks away from my house. While at the 7-11 convenience store, I did not buy candy like most other kids would do at my age; I spent most of my money playing the video arcade Dungeons and Dragons was my favorite. I loved it when the little white guy would get killed and turned into a skeleton. I seen this a lot because I was not able to master this game and it made me mad and I was addict. Sometimes, I was able trick the machine by putting a straw in the quarter slot, and once the straw hit the coin lever I instantly received extra credits, which allowed me to play for several hours. The store clerks knew what I was doing, but they did not care, since I was at the store almost every day and didn't cause any trouble. During this time in my life seemed as though time had stopped and I would forever be a kid, and I knew these moments would always be something that I would be able to reflect on later in life.

My days of playing fisherman in the creek and playing arcade games at the store were coming to an end. Yes, summer ended and a new school year began.

At a young age I truly had manifested a special relationship with GOD. At the age of three, the Bible was the first book that I remember getting off of my mother's cherry oak nightstand by her bed. I could read and pronounce most of the words, but did not understand some of the meanings. GOD was with me, because I would pray for him to give me the wisdom and knowledge to read this holy book. I always seen my name and birth date on the first page and believed that this was my personal copy. However, my lack of knowledge or illiteracy did not prevent me from feeling the warm nurturing presence from the Lord.

GOD's presence assured me that I always had someone to protect and believe in me. Before I went to bed at night I always said the Lord's Prayer. After I prayed, "Our Father which art in heaven. Hallowed be thy name-----". I then asked the Lord to take all those things that were not about Him and for Him out of my life, so that I could always remain focused on Him and His will.

Also that night I said an extra prayer that GOD would walk with me the next day because tomorrow also signaled a fresh beginning at new elementary school and I was entering the first grade at. As I lay in bed, I was so excited about meeting new friends and learning new things, it was hard for me to calm down and relax so that I could fall asleep. My new elementary school, Houston Elementary was the only school in Dove Springs and most of the students walked to school.

When I reached age seven and started the second grade, it was the first time I can remember a physically abusive confrontation involving my stepfather. Going to school every day allowed me to escape all the problems and pressures that I was having at home. The unforeseen pressures of why my mom was always crying, about unpaid light bills, the mortgage note or just praying to allow her money to stretch so she could put food on the table. Even though I was a kid I still inherited

THE BEGINNING

worrying atmosphere from my mother because I wanted to see my mom happy and smiling. Through GOD's blessing and mercy we made it with just the necessity of basic living. The simple things in life are sometimes taken for granted and we are trained today that we need all the material things of the world to live a GOOD LIFE. But all a person really needs is GOD's love, mercy, and grace.

It was during my sixth grade year that I started to experience the rough roads of life. It was time for me to stop being a kid and to grow up. Because I learned from my mother that the only way to live a purpose filled life is to have GOD in your life and let him carry your burdens and fight your battles.

Growing up during the early 80's most elementary schools ended when a student reached the sixth grade. There was no graduation ceremony and no books to sign. Most students were excited because they would be moving to Junior high school and elementary was now for babies. So the summer after I completed the sixth grade, I decided that I wanted to go to college and play football. Moving on to junior high school leaving elementary school behind was scary at first, but I looked forward to the breaks in between my classes and walking to my different classes.

The sixth grade for me was not only that I made it to this grade it also meant that I was growing up and I started to discover new things about me. My body change and my feeling about girls also change. Girls were more interesting to me now and I did not know how to deal with these emotions. My first crush and experienced a broken heart would happen during this school year. All of the sixth grade classes were taught in trailers outside the main school building, because of the rapid growth in the Dove Springs community.

LIVING 2 DIE OR DYING 2 LIVE

Her name was Kendra and her family had just moved to the neighborhood. Kendra's father was in the Air Force and had been stationed at Bergstrom AFB. When Kendra made her grandiose entry by opening the squeaky wooden trailer door, the class room started to feel more and more like being in a slow motion movie. As my eyes stayed focused on her my body was paralyzed and I could not move, because she was unknowingly seducing me with every movement. Kendra was tall for her age and she was of mixed race black and Asian with the prettiest brown skin and black hair I had ever seen. As she started to bend down to take her seat in her desk, I noticed that she was seated next to my best friend Ronald.

Kendra never knew I had a crush on her, because I could never muster enough courage to ask for her number. Even if I did get her number, I just knew that I would not be able to talk to her, because I could hardly speak whenever she was around me. My best friend Ronald got the privilege of being seated next to her in class. Ronald also got to become good friends with her and talked to her a lot during class. They even talked on the phone with each other with me listening, which I dreaded with each word. Keeping my silence and holding my breath with every moment that was spent on the phone, because I was in fear that they would start to ask each other, "the do u like me" conversation.

I did not tell Ronald my feelings for Kendra, because I knew that he would surely tell her and make a big spectacle about my crush on her. Ronald did feel that I had some feeling for her because of my facial reactions and sweaty palms whenever she came around.

Ronald and I met in the sixth grade and became friends instantly when we started to talk about the things we liked

THE BEGINNING

to do after school and becoming the number 1 ladies man in our class.

Football was the major thing that we had in common and we both played on the neighborhood little league football team that met at Houston elementary football field every evening after school. Dove Springs Cyclones was the name of the team which consisted of just the kids that ran around in the neighborhood. Our team did not initially have a great number of star football players, because this was the first year of any organized sports in our neighborhood. Our official games that we played took place early Saturday mornings at a football field on the eastside of town. Most of our games were against teams from the east and southwest side of town. My first official football game took place at Keiling Jr. High School football field that was man made on the top of a hill.

As the white van that I was riding in approached the parking lot I could see the football field in the distance and started to get butterflies in my stomach. This feeling was very new to me and I kept trying to turn it off and a get my game face on. When the van stopped and the door open we jumped out with just our football pants and Nike football shoes on, while carrying our helmets that were inside our shoulder pads. Coach Brown brought the entire team into a huddle to give us a Rick Flare WWF speech before kickoff. "Men we are here today to start a winning tradition for Cyclone football. I need all of you to dig deep and play with pride and show the other team that we mean business." As I digested Coach Brown's words, I began to feel the nervous nerves again that felt like literally butterflies were in my stomach. Our performance on the field did not match the intensity that we showed before the game. We suffered our first defeat and continued our losing streak for the rest of the football season.

LIVING 2 DIE OR DYING 2 LIVE

When the football season ended, early on Saturday mornings and during the evenings on the weekends I could always be found on my elementary school's outdoor basketball courts. I was too young and not good enough yet to play with the older boys, but they would let me play whenever they lacked enough players to form a team. My job on the team was to pass the ball inbound to other players, which I did not mind because, I was proud like a badge of honor to be playing with the older boys on the basketball court.

The little time that was spent at home, was usually to watch a great deal of football games on TV and always enjoyed watching Tony Dorsett score touchdowns for the Dallas Cowboys. I also watched collegiate football games; my favorite college team to watch was the University of Texas.

On some Saturdays when the Longhorns played at home, my friends and I would sneak into the Longhorn's stadium. The Longhorn football players gathered at the entrance to the field and waited until all of their teammates were out of the locker room. The players looked like giants to me. My friends and I would then work our way through the crowd until we were in a position to snatch the Longhorn players' towels from the front of their waist belts. Some of the towels came out easily and other towels that were hard to pull free, seemed like they were tied to the waist belt. So, after a few tugs on the players' towels, we release our grips and took off running to find a place to hide, because we knew that the stadium security force was on to us and was on their way to catch us and through us out of the stadium.

I collected the sport pages from the Austin American Statesman newspaper and with my steel scissors from my school supplies box, cut out pictures of football players and

THE BEGINNING

taped them to my bedroom walls. Then I would shut my eyes and imagine playing in the big stadiums where the collegiate and professional football players played their games. I knew if I worked hard on and off the field my dream would come true. I started watching the position I played in little league to see how the big league players played during football games. I picked up some of their good habits and effective techniques, but was still too small to pull them off at my level of play.

Houston Elementary did not have a little league football team, but the school did start a basketball and volleyball team for fifth and six grade students.

The last day of the sixth grade finally arrived; I had planned to ask Kendra for her number at the end of the school year. So if she rejected me, I would not have to sit in the small trailer house classroom with her all day while my classmates got the pleasure of teasing me for having a crush on her. When my opportunity finally came to ask Kendra for her number I stood there frozen like a Popsicle and softly mumbled, "Have a great summer." My friend Ronald intervened and asked, Kendra if he could walk her home and she accepted. I was crushed; it felt like my heart jumped out of my chest and took off running to catch Kendra who had left me standing there numb and unable to move. The walk home that afternoon seemed to take forever; it usually took only ten minutes. Once there, I went straight to my room and bawled like a little girl. I had never felt like this before about anything or anyone. A couple of days into the summer, my heart began to recover and had a chance for me to put it back into my chest, and I started to feel better. I somehow got my hands on a TOO SHORT tape, and after hearing his philosophy on women I promised to never let

LIVING 2 DIE OR DYING 2 LIVE

a girl hurt me like that -- ever again. I was officially applying to the University of TOO SHORT and to the school of Pimpology in Oakland, California.

That summer ended up being the best summer of my young life I ever had. Once Kendra was off the brain, I rode my huffy bike every day, early in the morning to Mabel Davis swimming pool and stay until it closed. Many of the kids from the neighborhood and the surrounding area met at the pool; because that was one of the ways we escaped the Texas heat. My skin turned from a dark brown to a coal black from being in the sun and swimming in the pool every day. Some of my friends gave me the nickname of black, because my skin was now tanned from the summer sun rays and as black as the midnight sky.

3

I'm Just Feeling Myself

The summer vacation from school was almost over when my virginity first got tested by some older boys in the neighborhood that I grew up with and that I ran around with. We were still too young to make a name for ourselves, but was affiliated with the know hustlers in our neighborhood, so we took it upon ourselves to let the world know that we were the infamously brothers known as The Crew.

My first adult film was seen with The Crew and I was blown away with the actions of what the actors were doing in the sexual video. The positions they were getting in and how they were pleasing each other seemed to me that they were really hurting each other and screaming because of the pain that was being administered. I had never been with a girl like this and my facial expression and body language on alerted the Crew that I had never seen anything like this and tried my hardest to remain cool and collected like the older boys. They knew that I was still a virgin and were laughing at me on the inside, while only showing a hard smile on the outside. The Crew would always ask me sex related questions during our viewing of these movies to test my virginity status, which I would carefully and skillfully give the wrong answers. The Crew would then quickly counter with asking me the names of the girls that I claim to have had sex with, to throw curve ball questions at me and to catch me in the act of lying. When the pressure of them drilling me with these questions got too heavy, I would react in a split second and I would quickly compose my thoughts and answer them with the names of girls on TV shows. I did this because this was the only way I could provided security that they would never find these girls. I also knew these names would not come back to haunt me later.

Watching these Adult movies with The Crew transitioned into a everyday thing the more these movies became available to us. The more I watched the sexual tapes the more curious I became. My mind was like a sponge recording the information that I was seeing with my eyes. Questions raced through my head wondering where did that white stuff was coming from that was leaking out of the man's penis; it was like the man was pissing on the women while screaming and sweating. The only thing that came out of my private area was the yellow liquid. My question about the white stuff remained a question because of my fear being teased by The Crew.

My first summer kiss never happened. The only opportunity that I did have I blew it, because I chickened out and was too scared to go into the room where my sister's friend was anxiously waiting for me. Subconsciously I kept hearing my mom voice telling me that if I kissed this girl that she was going to get pregnant and I would have to drop out of school and get a job to support her and the baby. Her name was Nikki and she lived next door; Nikki and my sister played together all the time. When I was around Nikki, she would stop playing with my sister and always wanted to play house, but once again

I'M JUST FEELING MYSELF

I would chicken out. Nikki, my sis, and I did lots of things together, because we were the only kids on our block. I remember watching my first horror flick at Nikki's house, "Friday the 13th":, Jason had me scared for weeks after I saw the movie; he was always chasing after me in my dreams.

I never made a move on Nikki, not because I did not want to, but because I did not know what to do and was scared of being laughed at.

On some Saturday nights the Crew and I would meet at the neighborhood skating rink to practice our pickup skills on the girls in attendance and to show off our latest break dancing moves. During the late '80s the break dancing craze in America had exploded, and many parents had temporary relief knowing were their kids were. Parents were happy that their children were participating break dancing moves instead of strong-armed robbery moves. There was always a big crowd at the skating rink, because most of the break dancing crews from other neighborhoods would come to compete with our side of town. When the break dancing battle was over the roller skates were taken off and we danced until the rink closed. Many of the kids got picked up by their parents. I always made excuses for my parents, because I knew that they were not going to pick me up. Sometimes I had to walk home. But I did not care, because going to the skating rink was well worth the 10-mile walk.

4

Walk With Me LORD

On some Sunday mornings I would wake up with a smile and a song in my heart and certain pep in my step. Even though I had been out the night before, I would still get excited when I read my bible and would have the opportunity to share what I read in Sunday school. At a very early age I had manifested a true relationship with GOD and also knew the power of GOD and how His teachings and beliefs affect peoples' lives.

My stepfather and mother had been brought up in the church; my stepfather was the son of a prominent reverend in the community. This would not be the first time that I woke up early on Sunday morning and got myself dressed and walked to Teri Road Baptist Church. My parents were too tired to go to church on most Sunday mornings because they stayed out all night parting and drinking at the Chicken Shack on the Eastside of town. My stepfather was the pianist in a soul band called the Funk Masters.

The band practiced in our garage and would leave their equipment; I did try to play most of the instruments, but stopped because of my fear of breaking them. I had fallen in love with music from that point and the band gave me the experience to know what live good music sounded like.

With just a white tee shirt and some old pair of blue jeans I continued going to Teri Road Baptist church until the family that invited me moved out of our neighborhood. My friend before he left invited me over his house and gave me a pair of football shoes that smelled like old cigars and told me that I would do big things with these shoes. I knew that was GOD talking to me through him.

This also began a trend of how people would come into my life for a while and then leave. I never understood why people always left me, without a word of explanation. This was also them time that I started to developed problems with abandonment issues with people that I met, which translated into a phobia regarding me staying at home alone.

During my adolescence my parents had little involvement with my growth into a young adult and my school education. They primarily focused on my sister, because she was the child they had created together. The only time my parents did pay attention to me was during sessions of abuse. I was the only proud participant, as my sister did not receive this brand of discipline. Sometimes I got a beating just to remind me of the power that my stepfather had over me. The mental abuse did not affect me that much, because I had a solid foundation in GOD, and knew what the Bible said about my situation. "That trouble is only temporary and does not last." I often prayed for my parents to change their ways and for us to become a normal, loving family. I got so many beating that my tears dried up and I would just pretend to cry. I never fought back because the Bible taught me that a child should always honor their mother and father so their days on this earth will be long. I also did not want to get punished by GOD for fighting back, so I took the beatings like a man. My mother also in a cynical way would reinforce the scripture of honoring your parents, but then would show that she knew that their treatment of me was wrong by asking me not to tell anyone about the beatings.

At this time in my life GOD was the only friend I had. I constantly reminded myself of His promise -- that He loved me and would fight my battles. In the fifth grade I stopped coming home after school, and stayed out long enough until I thought my parents were asleep. The reason I did this is because I felt if my parents did not see me they could not beat me. So, when I did decide to come in for the night I hoped my parents would have retired to the bedroom. Unfortunately, they would often wait until I fell asleep and wake me up with a host of whippings from a leather belt. My mother's way of getting her two cents in would be to wait until I got in the shower and then surprise me with her brown extension cord.

I was forced to work for everything that I received and started hustling for money at the age of 10. I would walk around the neighborhood with a lawn mower and gas can and go door-to-door offering my services. There were yards that only took about 15 minutes to cut, and then there were yards that were clean in the front, but when I went to cut the back yard it was like I had stepped into *Jurassic Park*. I remember one yard where the grass was so high that I could not even get into the backyard. My stepfather had to come and cut the grass for me. This was one of the few times my stepfather looked out for me. Cutting grass in the Texas summer heat got old real fast, but I made good money for a 10 year-old kid. I have always had an entrepreneurial spirit and knew that the only way that I would make a large sum of money was to start my own business. When you work for a company, the company will work your tongue out, and once the company wrings all of the productivity out of you, you wind up with a pink slip. In so many cases, the company waits for you to become eligible for retirement and then finds a reason to replace you with a younger more desperate worker, who they can pay half your salary. My mother drove school buses for 21 years until she grew ill, and she was forced into early retirement. Considering the years that my mom sacrificed driving school buses, financially it appeared as though she had not worked a day in her life. My mother basically lived from paycheck to paycheck, and was the main provider for the family. She was always under a tremendous amount of stress trying to pay all the bills alone.

My stepfather was notorious for playing the field and always left my mother at home with my sister and me. My stepfather was the type of person who took money out of his household; so that he could entertain women, and give the false impression that he had money. My stepfather was a man who always dreamed of making it big, but never truly succeeded at anything.

My mother worked hard and always had a giving heart; she would lend money to family members and for those same family members to turn their backs on her when she needed them really tore her apart. I know now why my mom pushed me away; she did it so that I could live my dreams and not get caught in poverty's revolving door. The journey of becoming a man started early and life's pressures and stressors already had their grips on me.

5

Do The Right Thing

I had to grow up faster than other children my age. Coming from a very dysfunctional atmosphere, I continually got on my knees and prayed for my family to become as one, and to truly and wholeheartedly love one another. God was prevalent in my life, but I would sometimes stray from His teachings, if certain people were around.

When I started Junior high school I had probably been involved with more criminal activity -- without getting caught -- than a career criminal, including breaking the three strikes law. My older cousin, who greatly influenced my life of crime, always took me around his friends. Most of the time I just went along and participated in the criminal acts, because I did not want to embarrass my cousin in front of his friends, or listen to them call me a punk and be banished from them. I would subconsciously pray the whole time that we indulged into unlawful things, so that GOD would protect us and not let us get caught. I looked forward to the weekends that I was allowed to spend at my cousin's house. It gave me a chance to get away from my parents' house, where I always had to follow

DO THE RIGHT THING

strict rules and was sometimes disciplined for things that I did not do.

There was one time that I remember that my sister made a bet with me that she could get me a beating whenever she wanted to. So I took her up on her offer, and as my parents entered the front door of our house after being out all day. My sister started crying and said that I had hit her. I did not have a chance to explain my side of the story. I was immediately dealt an open-handed slap by my stepfather. I should have seen that one coming.

My cousin lived on the north side of town and I resided on the south side. During 1986 there was truly no conflict between the North and South side of the city. The division between north and south commenced when the movie "Colors" came out. The fallout from the movie was as though my city had received a lethal injection of gang activity. I lost numerous friends. The north side gang was known as "The "Crips", and the gang on the south side was called "The Bloods".

There was one time that I faintly remember, while visiting my cousin for the weekend. My cousin's friends had decided to steal a school bus and drive it to the projects to meet some girls, and to take care of some business. The master plan was to steal the school bus at midnight when the streets of Austin would be devoid of heavy traffic. Even though Austin is the capital of the big state of Texas, it felt like a small town to the minorities in the city. I did not want to go through with this because I knew what would happen if we got caught: my dreams of going to college and playing football for the University of Texas would be impossible. And yet, with so much peer pressure, there was no way I could refuse to participate in this criminal caper. My involvement in this crime would also prove that I was down for anything; it would solidify my membership with my cousin friends.

LIVING 2 DIE OR DYING 2 LIVE

While I stepped onto the school bus, I instantly went into prayer mode and asked GOD to let us make it safely without any cops to the PJ's. On arrival at the PJ's, we ditched the small bus in a field. A few days later I saw the school bus on the local news ("Crime Stoppers"); the police had discovered a school bus in a field. Law enforcement had also issued a reward on "Crime Stoppers" and petitioned the community for any information on how the bus got there. While watching the news story, I got down on my knees and thanked GOD, because I knew at that point that a life of crime was not for me.

I was never a fan of intrigue the glamour of the fast life or the money that accompanied it. Some of my uncles, cousins, and friends that took this route and they always ended up worse off than they were before. My cousin, who was by now a seasoned criminal and continuously stayed in and out of prison, seemed like he could not shake the grip that the streets had on him. "If a person does not earn their possessions, they will never truly respect or value them."

The time spent with my cousin and his friends did end as I got older and I realized that I had to choose a path in life that was different from my cousin, because instant success via the wrong path never lasts. Furthermore, I wanted something that would endure not only throughout my lifetime, but also for my kids and generations to come.

As the summer of 1984 came to an end I was excited to be starting my last year of junior high school. Two weeks before school commenced I started going to the University of Texas track to get into shape for the football season that would begin on the first day of Junior High school. There was no 2 a day summer football training for Junior High school, the football training always started when the class started at the school. I self-trained. The prior Fulmore Junior High season we won the

DO THE RIGHT THING

city championship, and I was excited at the prospect that we could win it again. I planned to be ready to make it happen.

    A quiet and peaceful morning in September 1985 I could smell the scent of fresh cut grass and the smell of young girls perfumes, as we waited for our bright yellow school bus pulled up to A. T. Fulmore Junior High School, I had earned my stripes and now I was first in the food chain instead of last as a seventh grader. I could now walk the halls with my chest out and chastise the new seventh graders as I had been chastised by the eighth graders, who had moved on to high school.

    During the assembly the Crew and I looked through the crowd that was in the bench seats in the gymnasium. We targeted and plotted on the seventh graders who were from our neighborhood, so we would not have to worry about revenge. The principal gave his WWC speech and acknowledged that this would be a special year at Fulmore Junior High school, because the school was celebrating 100 years of existence. A. T. Fulmore Junior High School was originally known as Austin Ward School, a one-room box house that had a water system consisting of a barrel filled with water from the Colorado River, and covered with a gunnysack. The principal also addressed the new football season, and the fact that our team had already made a place for another district champion trophy. All the students started to cheer and there was great excitement in the air. I was one of a few seventh graders who made the district championship team last year. I mostly cheered my fellow eighth grade teammates to victory from the sideline. I had dreamed of being a good running back like Tony Dorsett, but I later found out when I got to high school that God had decided my talents were best suited to defense at defensive end.

I saw very little playing time but never got discouraged, because I knew that football was the sport that would get me to college and maybe to the National Football League (NFL). The year prior the Austin Independent School District implemented for the first time the infamous,

"no pass no play rule". This rule had a huge impact on student athletes and forced them to be good students and athletes. The old saying that jocks were dumb went out the window when the no pass no play rule came into effect.

My eight-grade junior high school football season did not turn out as we had planned. Our team destroyed and shut out our first two opponents. For the next four football games, we were only able to pull out one win -- ending our season with a .500 record. Most of my teammates looked forward to the pizza parties after the games. The local pizza restaurant was in walking distance from Fulmore Junior High School. My teammates and I would meet up with the other students from school to celebrate. I did not matter if we won or lost the game, there was a party.

When the disappointing football season finally ended our team took the time to reflect and evaluate what was needed to become a winning team. Most of the players that were on my eighth grade team would be attending the same high school the following year.

In November 1985, basketball tryouts started. I was naïve enough to think because I played on the football team that I had a spot on the basketball team, since the same person coached both sports. I entered basketball tryouts without giving my all and was rewarded with being cut from the tryouts. I was in a state of shock for a while. On the other hand I did not hang my head, as basketball was not the sport that I chose to make me rich. I did play basketball in a community league, where I scored 19 points in a playoff loss to a cross-town rival.

DO THE RIGHT THING

Junior high had a different feel when I returned to school from winter break, which had given me time to think about how I would survive if I did not make it to the National Football League. I had noticed that I was a natural in my math classes and my teachers did, as well. I never really studied or did the homework, but seemed to somehow pass my tests. I knew that I wanted to be a successful business professional, but did not know in what capacity. After talking to my math teacher I chose the field of accounting and never looked back.

By the Spring of 1986 hormones and love were in the air, and I decided that I needed to get a jump start on all of my male classmates by selecting girls who were already my friends, and who would say yes when I asked them to the eighth grade dance. So I asked several girls for their number and started the process of elimination. I narrowed my selection in a couple of weeks to one girl, but when she was asked by her female friends, she told them that she was going to the dance with no one. I did not get upset, I just called the girl that I had on backup; we had a great time at the dance and everyone there were looking at us, as we pulled up in our limousine.

The eighth grade prom and the last eighth grade dance of the year were one in the same. Here was the highlight of my eighth grade year, because the dance signified the rite of passage to high school. The dance was the last social event where I would see most of my eight grade friends as many of us would be moving on to different high schools. We said goodbye with a bang.

With school over, I returned to my favorite swimming hole. That summer my virginity was tested again. Most of the single parents that could not afford a summer program for their children left their teenagers at home all day with the oldest child in charge. Most of the kids who stayed at home were girls, many of whom were around my age. Some were older. There were two good friends from the Crew that I grew up with who knew most of the girls in my neighborhood.

"Q" was sort of the bully in the group; he shook down anyone who had money. Oddly, Q went on to become one of the top running backs at his high school and in his district.

Bruno was more of the player type, who always had the latest gear and was always about his money. The first time I smoked weed with Bruno, I was laughing so much that I had to stay at his house until I could regain my composure. Bruno and I ran around quite a bit in the hood and were well known. One day I was chilling at his house like we always did during summer vacation. Bruno's cousin showed us a .380-caliber pistol that he had just acquired; and gave us a demonstration of how it worked. After showing us how to load the pistol, he took us into the backyard and discharged one round. I realized that when a hustler has to buy a pistol for protection, that hustler is dealing with large amounts of money and product. In short, buying a pistol is necessary to protect your investment and advance your game.

Q, Bruno, and I called some girls during the night to set up an orgy during the day when their parents left for work. I was still green in the area of kissing a girl, so having sex with one was definitely off the agenda. Q and Bruno were very experienced in having sex with girls and they indulged often. The daytime orgy was set up with a female that we all knew would be down for a train. Q and Bruno invited me to tag along like I always did because my curiosity antennas were up. When we approached the duplex there was a clear path to the door, because the girl mom's car was missing from the driveway. The white front door opened and I started to hear my mother's voice again and her philosophy of what would happen to me if I had sex with a girl and got her pregnant. She informed me that I would have to drop out of school, get a job, and take care of the girl and the baby. Those words rang in my head and killed any sexual thought I had when I was around any girl who gave me the slightest impression that they wanted to take it to that level.

As Q entered the girl's bedroom where the girl was laying in the bed with no clothes on, he purposely left the door cracked so that we could see him having sex with her. I grew so scared that I became sick and had to leave the house to get some air, because I felt like I was going to pass out. I waited and stayed outside until Q and Bruno finished their business. As we left the house they just looked at me and smiled, but nothing was said or ever brought up about me chickening out on the train.

I really started to think about girls and sex as I grew older, but there was nobody to ask about the birds and bees without suffering embarrassment. Much of my learning about the other sex was hands on and by trial and error. Each time a girl rejected me, my game got stronger and more refined, because what worked and what did not became clearer and clearer.

Girls my age liked to talk on the phone for hours and hours so I became a good listener. The more I listened to girl gossip the better equipped I became when I approached one. The things that I can pinpoint about young teenage girls are -- they thrive on gossip, drama, competition, and are more mischievous than boys. Gossip is something that girls are born with and it seems to flow through their veins. To keep the gossip going there has to be some form of drama afoot -- good or bad. Good drama is when a girl can keep her girlfriends entertained with her stories or factual concepts that hurt no one in their clique of friends, and stays within the group. Then, there is the common drama that happens between boyfriend and girlfriend.

LIVING 2 DIE OR DYING 2 LIVE

The bad drama is displayed like a person auditioning for a movie script before a live audience. The majority of bad drama stems from what somebody said about a person and what that person plans to say about it in front of their audience of casting directors. The other part of bad drama is when it intensifies and results in emotional and often physical harm to the main characters involved in the bad drama.

The competition between girls and the competition between boys really starts when they reach adolescence. The reason for competition between the two groups, I believe, is the desire to be popular. Another competition entails winning the attention of the best looking guy/girl in the school and keeping that person's attention, while fighting off other potential threats.

The various popularity contests never interested me, nor did I really care what people thought about me, because I treated all my friends the way I wanted to be treated. They knew me to be was a very loyal person, who would take most of their secrets to my grave.

I grew both spiritually and psychologically while in junior high and gradually formed into the person I would become as an adult. Starting the next chapter of my life as a high school student was exciting. I learned in junior high that some people might befriend you because they believe that there is something to gain from the friendship. These types of friends should be given enough rope to hang themselves when the time comes. A true friend will have your back through the good and bad times. That friend should always have encouraging words and a positive attitude in and out of your presence. This friend should be a good advisor and must always render a truthful response to any question, even if it hurts you. Tough love is enlightening. A friend will always be your friend, but a foe will only be in your life to take advantage of you.

Just because you may have grown up with a person does not make them a friend. There may be some negativity harbored by this person, which they never told you, because they benefited from the association in some way. For example, say a teenager gets a car. When that teenager's friends find out that the teenager has wheels, so-called friends will come out of the woodwork. Always remember the people who were there when you all had to catch that city bus in the rain and cold. Beware of the other sex that ignored you before you got your car that suddenly considers you to be worthy of their company. These are some of the things that filled my thoughts during the summer before I started - high school.

6

"Young Macaronii"

The first year of high school was great and I was maturing as will a normal teen. My hormones started to kick in, but I never let it overtake me, because I truly knew little about the opposite sex. My high school ride started at William B. Travis High School in Austin, Texas and I played on the freshman football and basketball teams. Participating in high school sports kept me in shape and took my mind off the girls. When I reached 9th grade, I was still a virgin, and would get extremely nervous when girls I liked or had a crush on came around me.

That summer I had to decide which high school in Austin would give me the best chance to prepare for a football scholarship. The guys on my freshman team had been my teammates since junior high school, and we treated each other as brothers. Our freshman record was 9-1 and the team had some great athletes, but that summer some redistricting of school zones transpired, and because of where I lived, I was forced to attend another school in the district. To this day I truly missed playing with those guys and rooted for them when they made the state playoffs our senior year in high school.

"YOUNG MACARONII"

A neighbor of mine was already attending Austin High School and he convinced me that Austin was the best school for my talents. The following school year, I enrolled at Stephen F. Austin High School. During this time in my life some of the wheels of my high school ride came off. Austin High had a different atmosphere, one that I had never before experienced. When the bell rang students literally ran to class. They wanted to make good grades, and unlike at other schools -- Austin's students who excelled at their studies never got teased. Also, there was no peer pressure to be popular or hang with a crew. A student could be whatever they wanted to be. Austin High showed me what school was all about and how far behind I was. I never did any homework; I would do it in class or go to the school library during lunch. I remember the first time that I had to write a research paper. I was blown away. In my previous English and reading classes we only had to write short stories, which were due at the end of class. There was no research, books to read, citing authors, footnotes; it was as though the teacher spoke a new language.

Once I got into the flow of what my teachers expected of me, things seemed to get a little easier.

During my tenth grade year the relationship with my stepfather intensified, and I started to leave home again and stay out most of the night in the streets. I thought of myself as a nightwalker.

The atmosphere at Austin High greatly appealed to me; it was also a blessing that I met who would become my best friend – Kevin. We had so much in common that we often joked that we were born of the same mother. Kevin was also new to Austin High School, having transferred - from Baton Rouge, LA. My biological father was also from Louisiana, so we clicked instantly. Kevin lived with his grandmother along with his cousins. Grandma N was the sweetest lady, but was very strict about the rules of her house. She did not like for anyone to tie up her home phone "talking to nappy-headed girls." There was a one-minute time limit that lasted about ten seconds before she ordered you off her phone. If, Kevin did not instantly hang up, Grandma N would get on the line and inform Kevin that his time was up and to say goodbye. Before calling any girls, we tried to wait for Grandma N to go to sleep, but she would wake up on cue to check her line and order Kevin off her phone.

Grandma N always made me feel welcome at her house. Whenever she cooked dinner Grandma N always offered me something to eat, even though she had a house full of grandchildren to feed. Grandma N saw something in me and with her motherly instincts knew that I had come from an unpleasant household. I used to joke with Grandma N and tell her --, "When I grow up I am going to marry you". That line would always get her smiling and laughing.

Grandma N started calling me her boy and always cooked me a meal or cake during my visits home on military leave. I did not get a chance to say goodbye when she died, but I knew she was smiling from heaven when I showed up at her house looking for her. Grandma N is now looking down on Kevin and I saying to Kevin, "get off my phone" and to me "that's my boy". I will always love and remember you, Grandma N.

Kevin and I went to the mall on Saturdays to sharpen up our Mack Daddy game on the ladies. During the last semester of tenth grade my stepdad and I had a huge argument that led to a physical fight. I was not a little boy anymore -- I was a strong 16 year-old athlete. I hit my step-dad so hard that he flew through the front door and nearly tore the screen door of its hinges. I simply could not take any more of his foolishness.

"YOUNG MACARONII"

My mother pled with me to stop, so I did and left with the clothes on my back. My mom then decided it was best for me to permanently leave her house, so I left a place that was never home for me and caught a greyhound bus in the middle of the night to my grandmother's house in Waco, Texas.

My grandmother was very receptive when I arrived at her house and immediately laid down the rules. The next morning I caught the school bus and enrolled in Waco High School and was able to start spring football training with the varsity football team.

Waco had a small town feel to it; everyone knew everyone, or they were all related to each other. There was little to do in Waco, other than get into mischief. On some night's my cousin and his friends would sneak up behind cars at the only stop light in town and scare the drivers while they sat at the light. The stop light scaring stopped when a guy that we scared, chased us for blocks in his old pickup truck before giving up. My cousin's family decided to move to Waco a year before, because of the cheap rent and housing market. Weekends I spent at my cousin's house, because my grandmother did not allow me to come home late at night. On some Saturday evenings dances were held at the Dewey Community Center, which nearly every kid in Waco attended. The local singing groups would show up and put their talents on display. The most famous known singing group that signed a major record deal from Waco, Texas went by the name of Hi-Five. Hi-Five was a group of young boys who were in junior high school that caught the attention of a record label. Waco High School was the pride of the city and the residents supported the school. When the school year ended I returned to my parents' house after my mother apologized; and though, the situation with my step-dad was still tense, the beatings stopped.

LIVING 2 DIE OR DYING 2 LIVE

January 1990, I started my last semester of high school at Austin High. I had to accept the harsh reality that I was not going to college. My high school grades were not good enough to be accepted at any four-year university, but I did not feel sorry for myself, because, that meant that plan B would be implemented. I planned to attend the local community college until my GPA improved, and then transfer to a major university.

During our senior year in high school, my friend Kevin and I had joined a youth organization called Delteens sponsored by the sorority "Delta Sigma Theta." The sessions I attended for the Delteens opened my eyes about never giving up and to always work hard at whatever you decide to do in life and good things will follow.

The speaker at one Delteens session announced that the Delteens would spend spring break in Tennessee to visit some HBCU's in the Memphis and Nashville areas. Wow, this would be my first trip out of Texas; I was very excited. However, I had less than a month to raise the money to go. The other Delteens had already appropriated funds, because unlike me, they had been in the organization for the entire school year. Raising the money to go on the spring break trip was impossible, due to my parent's noninvolvement with me. I knew that they would not even consider giving me the money. So, I broke the bad news to my friend Kevin, that I would not be able to make the trip. But Kevin insisted that I just show up and get on the bus.

The night before the trip I prayed to my heavenly father that I needed Him to make a way for me to make the bus trip to Tennessee. That Friday night/early Saturday morning I showed up with bags packed and no money in my pockets. I knew that I was supposed to be on the bus, and that GOD had already made a place for me. Kevin was very happy that I came, and offered to share with me the money that his grandmother had given him for food. God makes a way when it seems like there are none in the natural world.

In route to Tennessee one of the lady chaperons, who was a Delta, got wind that I was on the trip with no money and had not paid for the privilege. The head chaperone on the trip, Mrs. Thompson, pulled me aside. I was very nervous; small bullets of sweat broke out on my forehead. I was afraid Mrs. Thompson was going to make a big scene. Instead, she smiled and told me that I had a person on the trip with us, who would pay for all my expenses and whenever I needed money for food to come and ask her for it. Thank You Jesus!!!! I was so happy when Mrs. Thompson told me that, and I made a promise to myself that I would always be grateful to Mrs. Thompson and the Delta Sigma Theta organization.

That is why I took the time to acknowledge the Delta's, because without their help the trip to Tennessee would have been a long trip without any food or money. It also instilled in me the importance of giving back, because you never know whose life you may be able to change. It was truly a blessing from GOD, that He spoke to this rare lady to help one of his children. This is also why I took the time to write a poem of appreciation and love to the Delta Sigma Theta Organization.

LIVING 2 DIE OR DYING 2 LIVE

"A Woman named Delta Sigma Theta"

You will always be a rare red diamond in my eyes

Even though we only met once when I was a young teen

The genuine nurturing spirit that you showed me helped to build my self-esteem

Your act of kindness has stayed with me and has with stood the test of time

My appreciation and love for you is greater than the love between a mother and her child

When I grow up I am going to buy you that red brick house on 1913 Founders Lane

Because I know that you are not into fortune or fame

Your acts of generosity are the reason why my dreams are now coming true

But please stand up and take a bow, because you are definitely about positive change

You have truly made a difference in my life and when I needed help you came

to help ease my growing pains

XOXOXOXOXOXOXOXO

Delteen 90'

7

Growing Pains

In June 1990, I graduated from Stephen F. Austin High School, with no concrete plans regarding my future. I had to immediately tighten up on what I wanted to do and how I was going to do it. During the early '90s Austin had become a place where trouble for young black men was easy to get into. It was hell to break free once you were in the hands of the police. My grades were atrocious and my GPA was only 1.4, though I always managed to be eligible to play football during the season. When the football season ended, so did the passing grades. I remember signing up for the school choir, because I thought in choir I would be able to receive an easy A. The choir class at my school was very good and would travel to complete in various contests, but I never went because I had to work. I explained this to my choir teacher, but he was unsympathetic and gave me an F for the semester. I had to sing with the choir at my high school graduation, which I hated. Thank GOD I did not need that class to graduate.

During track season of my senior year at Austin High, I met Monique and we began conversing on the phone. Monique was younger than me, but she was very mature for her age. I stood a lean 6'3" while she was only about 5 feet -- on a good day. Monique was a beautiful brown skinned girl with long beautiful hair. I used to joke with her that she had a different father, because she did not look like anyone in her family. Monique and I hit it off from the first time we talked and I truly believed that I had met my soul mate.

There were times that I was allowed to stay the night at her house, when I would purposely miss the last bus leaving from her neighborhood. I slept on the couch in the living room, but Monique would sit with me until early the next morning. Most of the time we would just chill and watch TV, and she would always rub my head until I was asleep. We had planned to always be together and would get married when she finished high school. My relationship with Monique blossomed quickly, because being with her felt like that was the place GOD wanted me to be.

In August 1990, I visited Austin Community College (ACC) to see if I could enroll and to see what the community college had to offer me. Even though my high school grades were not up to par, ACC allowed me to take college courses, and after two years if I maintained a B average I would be able to transfer to a four year college or university. When the time came to register I enrolled in the basic college courses and some foundation courses to help me elevate my GPA. When Monique and I finally started a life together, I wanted to be the man that was able to provide a nice a comfortable life for her. I thought that when I received a college degree the degree would allow me to get a job with a high enough salary, so that my wife Monique could stay at home when we started having children and raising our family.

Beginning a new chapter in my life and shutting the door

on the old one was exciting. But first I needed to get a car, because riding the bus around town gets old really quick. And even though riding the city bus allowed me to meet interesting people from all walks of life, it also took half the day to reach your destination. The city bus also served as my personal chauffeur during sightseeing trips. On days when I lacked anything to do I rode the city bus to wealthy neighborhoods, picked out my future home and slipped it into my personal memory file. This way, when I could afford the American dream house I already knew where I wanted to stay in Austin.

One afternoon, while riding the bus toward home, I met a lady who worked for the Texas State Bar Association. She had just gotten off work and noticed me as soon as she boarded the bus. We began to converse, and she asked if I had a job. Either I looked as though I needed a job or she was just looking out for me. "A blessing in disguise sent by my Lord." After our brief conversation, she said she was about to leave the State Bar and her boss was looking for a college student to be her executive assistant. I immediately jumped to my feet and with a big "Kool-Aid" smile, told her that I was the right person for the job. She then informed me of what I needed to bring the next day when I went to apply at the State Bar. Next, she promised to call her boss to alert him of my plans to complete an application. I thanked her for the opportunity and thanked GOD for the job.

This was the perfect job for me, because I could go to work in the morning and attend college at night. The Texas State Bar also had programs that would pay 75% of a college student's tuition. Things in my life were about to do an about face, as being employed at the Texas State Bar allowed me to be around positive and professional people. That night I could not sleep; I was beyond excited about my new job and working in downtown Austin. As I stepped off the city bus and saw the tall brown brick building I thought to myself "Am I dreaming?" I pinched myself just to make sure.

When I walked through the tall glass doors and into the atrium, I stepped into the elevator with the other employees and asked someone near the front to push the button for the executive suite. When the elevator opened on my floor clearly this was one of the doors GOD had opened for me. I introduced myself to the secretary, who escorted me to my future boss's office.

Mrs. Wells was a real cool lady and took an immediate interest in me. When she showed me my office I almost passed out, but then she told me that I would also be getting a pager. The only people I knew that had pagers were drug dealers. I later realized that the pager was given to me, so that my boss would always know where I was. But I did not care -- I was only 18 years old with my own office in downtown Austin. Whoo hoo!!.

I could not wait to tell Monique that her man was about to be like the man at the gas station. I was about to blow up!!!!! When most young college students my age found work they chose jobs that allowed them to work around their school schedules. Jobs for college students are limited and usually have no future after graduation. This job could have possibly inspired me to become a lawyer to protect the criminal and civil rights of the people. Actually, the salary was secondary to being in such a professional atmosphere, which was priceless.

Unfortunately, after a few weeks of catching the bus to work, attending night school and not getting enough rest, the schedule finally took its toll. I might have pulled it off with the support from my family. I only asked if they would pick me up from the north transit station when I got there around

11:30p.m. At this time of night there were no more buses going to our neighborhood. It took me a couple of hours to walk home, which left no opportunity for studying or sleep, since I had to get up at 5:00 a.m. to catch the bus. It took all of two hours to get to work, which only allowed 15 minutes before I started working. At 5:00 p.m. I left work and caught the bus to my first class, which started at 6:40 p.m. and ended at 10:00 p.m. I would call home for someone to pick me up at the transit station, but after a few hours of waiting I knew my parents were not coming. When I did speak to them on the phone, they would tell me that they were on their way but never showed up. When I continued calling them, they would take the receiver off of the hook; the line was busy for hours. On a few occasions, I even had Monique call my house to see if my parents would answer the phone; because when they knew I was calling to be picked up no one would answer the phone. But when I got paid, I had a personal chauffeur and my parents would ask me for money. My faith was once again tested and I know GOD does not want his people to act ugly, so I would just smile and get out of the car.

 The long walks home at night and not getting enough rest caused me to fall asleep at work and fall behind in my studies. My boss, Mrs. Wells even called me into her office for a heart to heart talk. During the conversation she would stress the importance of being dependable and showing up to work on time. I was also taking catnaps at work and she became aware of it, because I did not respond immediately to her pages. I did not tell her about my situation at home; I just stood there and listened to her advice. That was the last time that we talked, before I had signed up with an Army recruiter. I went to Mrs. Wells' office to say goodbye. I thanked her for her words of wisdom and for giving me the opportunity to work for her. I did not immediately tell Monique that I had talked to an Army recruiter, but she could sense that something was going on with me. I knew if I told her I was joining the Army that it was going to break her heart and that she might run away from home in order to me with me.

July 4, 1991 was Independence Day for the U.S., but it was my independence day, as well. I would be leaving all my troubles and starting a new chapter as a soldier in the United States Army.

Recently, on visiting Monique, I had noticed that she was always in bed or just waking up. She claimed exhaustion from summer school and track practice. I still had not told her that I was leaving soon for the Army. So on receipt of my last paycheck from the Texas State Bar, I rented a light blue Buick Cutlass to take Monique out on a date. My plan was to take her to the movies and later to dinner, but we never made it to either. Instead, we parked by the lake to watch the sunset. The atmosphere was quite romantic; we were finally alone to enjoy each other's presence.

While watching the sunset we started to cuddle and kiss. Monique had no idea that this might be our last kiss for a while, because I was shipping out to basic training in Anniston, Alabama at the end of the month. I planted kisses all over her petite body, while she rubbed hard on my back and arms. Then I looked into her eyes.

"Do you want me," I crooned.

And she responded "Yess!"

Without using protection, we made love until all of the water in our bodies sweated out. The motion in the ocean started and it got real good to her and me. Monique then told me not to pull out, the love making just felt so right.

A couple of weeks passed during which I stayed in touch

GROWING PAINS

with the Army recruiter, who soon informed me that it was time to go to San Antonio, Texas to choose my job in the Army and to be officially sworn in. I also had to have a physical. Having failed the eye exam, I was denied an infantry assignment. Being diagnosed as colorblind by the army doctors gave me one job choice and that was as an 88H Cargo Specialist. Basic training began on July 30 at Fort McClellan in Anniston, Alabama, which meant that it was necessary to leave Austin, Texas on July 29, 1991.

When I got back from San Antonio my recruiter picked me up from the bus station and dropped me off at home. When I entered through the door everyone looked surprised to see me, since I spent most of my time at Monique's house. My mother's generally bland expression turned to puzzlement; it was the look she wore whenever she was going to deliver unpleasant news. She took a deep breath. "You're eighteen years old now. You can't stay here anymore. Be a man and make your own way."

\At first I was startled, because I did not have anywhere else to go. Suddenly a sort of peace settled over me, and I just smiled, laughed and walked back out the door. Even though I was officially homeless, it kind of felt like I had been released from jail. My parents did not know that I had enlisted in the Army, until the day the army recruiter came to pick me up for basic training and I tendered them a very joyous goodbye.

When I got to Monique's house, I told her that she would not believe what had just happened. I recounted the scene at my parent's house. Monique looked at me, started to laugh, and said that I had been kicked out of my parent's house for a long time; I just did not know it.

The next day I went to the mall and got a credit card at one of the jewelry stores. I used my entire credit limit as soon as I was approved for the credit card by going on a shopping spree for Monique. I thought that if I gave her some nice jewelry and a promise ring that the gifts would quell the hurt she would feel after learning that I was enlisting with the Army. Things did not work out as planned, however, when I finally mustered the courage to tell Monique that I would be leaving for the Army in a few days.

"I don't want the gifts," she cried. "I just want to be with you . . . I want to go with you." The look in her eyes showed me that she truly cared about me and only me. That day I lost my best friend and lover. Monique cried every day until I left. I keep telling her that I would be back for her when I got to my permanent duty station. I tried my best to explain that I was going into the Army and that we could get married and live together after she finished high school. She closed her ears to my comments, and kept telling me that she was going to leave with me.

8

Recruit 2 Army Soldier

On July 29, 1991, I left Austin, Texas and boarded a bus to San Antonio; from there I was sent to basic training at Fort McClellan, Alabama. I had enlisted in the United States Army for four years. From San Antonio, I caught a flight to Atlanta, GA, where I waited for a government shuttle bus that transported new Army recruits to their basic training post. When I reached Atlanta the vibes were such that I felt like I belonged there.

While waiting for the government shuttle bus I met a young lady from Rochester, NY. After a few minutes of conversation it became clear that we had much in common. She was attending school in Atlanta and was going home for the weekend. I have always been a person to whom people confide their problems. I freely render advice when asked, but I mostly just listen. When the time came for us to depart for our respective destinations, I asked that she keep me in her prayers and promised to do the same for her. It is not just a coincidence, when you meet people who believe in the Lord. It is more like check points to keep you on the path of righteousness. The Lord has already prepared a prosperous destiny for unborn babies still in their mother's womb. As babies grow up and become adults, the Lord gives most of us a sound mind and the right to choose heaven or hell.

On the long ride from Atlanta to Anniston, Alabama I had a chance to get some much needed sleep. However, when I reached Fort McClellan in the early morning hours, I was immediately ordered out of the van and reported to the staging area for new recruits. Later that day we were divided into groups, which were then labeled from A-Z. "A" group was called Alpha Company and so on. Once we discovered what company we were in., they we reported to those companies for further processing. I was assigned to Bravo Co. and had to stand in line for the ceremonial shaving of the head by the barbershop inside the Exchange. When every head of hair was shorn, my company was ordered to board a yellow school bus that stood waiting outside. Bravo Company was transported to the barracks, where we would be housed for basic training. As we headed toward the barracks, I started to daydream about what might be going on back home with Monique, how she was holding up, and whether I made the right decision enlisting in the Army. Once the bus came to a complete stop, there was no turning back now. As the school bus doors swung open, in came a bevy of screaming drill sergeants ordering all of us to get off the bus pronto. There was mass confusion; some recruits lost their cool and minds the moment the screaming started. The drill sergeants then lined us all up, luggage in hand. Some of the new recruits seemed to be under the impression that basic training was going to be like a summer vacation, as they were toting a bulky luggage from their home. The drill sergeants swarmed over these recruits like a disturbed hornets' nest. It was funny to me, although I did not laugh or smile, because I was trying to stay under the drill sergeants' radar. The drill sergeants smelled weakness like sharks smell blood in the water. Their tactic of instantly putting fear into the new recruits, as they lined up off the bus – worked, since few of them had ever been talked to or treated this way. They took the screaming from the drill sergeants personal. I just tuned the drill sergeants out until they directed their questions or attention my way. The screaming had the same intensity of a football coach screaming at a player for screwing up on a play that had been practiced for a whole week.

I quickly analyzed the situation and came to the conclusion of that I had to remain all but invisible to the drill sergeants, while showing them that I was a natural leader. After a couple of weeks passed I became the leader of my platoon. This was the first time I had tested being in control. I took to the leadership role, like a fish to water, having always had a leadership mentality. Leading people or teammates was just second nature to me.

I was a disciplined motivator, because my platoon knew that I would stand up for them right or wrong. This quality helped me lead by example and built trust between my fellow recruits and me.

The best times in basic training were when recruits were allowed to use the phone to call home, and mail call at the end of the day. Most of the letters recruits received were from their girlfriends or wives. The letters from home allowed most recruits to escape from the pressures of basic training. They read their letters and reminisced about the good times they spent with that special person back home. These letters were treasured by recruits in the same way that I treasured books from the Bible. The letters also helped recruits get through the hard times. There were good letters and the infamous Dear

LIVING 2 DIE OR DYING 2 LIVE

John letters informing an unlucky recipient that his hometown girlfriend had become the town slut, or that she had run off with the recruit's best friend. I can say this for Monique -- she kept me in check with her frequent cards and letters. I did not get a Dear John letter, but I did get a letter telling me to call home as soon as possible.

When I got the opportunity to use my phone time I called Monique. She did not sound happy on the phone; something in her tone signaled to me that all was not well. Finally, in an unsettling voice, she explained why she was always tired and sleeping so much. She was pregnant. Monique -- at age 16 -- was four months pregnant. Those words went through my body like lightning bolts. She asked me what I wanted to do about the pregnancy. My world had stopped. Time was at a standstill, waiting for me to respond to Monique's question so that it could start up again. This was definitely a time in my life that any decision I made on this subject would greatly affect me forever, whether it was to keep the baby, or abort the baby. Monique was only 16, and had not graduated from high school, but was very mature about the pregnancy. She would not have given having the child a second thought if I had been in Austin, Texas by her side. I did not want her to become a statistic, and so after a couple of weeks discussing the pregnancy, I told her that I wanted to have the child, but we should also think about her age and what her parents would say and do to us. Monique's parents were devout Seventh Day Adventists, and when Monique's mom found out about Monique's pregnancy, Monique was forced to have an abortion, which tore her apart and strained our relationship.

I had just completed a month in basic training when the next phase of the process began. It consisted of two weeks of field training and simulated war games in the forest, where we

RECRUIT 2 ARMY SOLDIER

set up a campsite. Early in the morning on what would be another hot summer's day in Alabama, the drill sergeants' road marched all the platoons in Bravo Company to the field training location on the base, while the platoons chanted the Army's finest marching songs. "Jody got your girl and gone" and "My recruiter told me," were classic marching songs and were relevant then and now. When we finally reached the campsite, the drill sergeants divided us into our respective platoons. My platoon's drill sergeant advised us to partner up with someone, because the tent that we were issued was just half a tent. Each recruit chose another recruit, so that the two recruits could assemble a whole tent. Once all the tents were set up, we were ordered to dig a trench around our tents, because the trench would stop the heavy rain water from flowing into the tent. The flowing water would instead go into the trenches and flow around the tents instead of flooding out the entire tent and being carried away by the flowing rain water. Spending time in the outdoors tested your manhood and separated the boys from the men. This was also a test by the Army to teach use survival skills in case we were ever put in this type of environment or situation.

Sleeping under the stars was relaxing, after being in the hot and blazing Alabama sun all day. On the last night of field training all the platoons in Bravo Company were briefed that on this night the field training would take place with on the ground simulated war games. The nighttime field training was a mock nighttime ambush by the enemy. Successful would be measured by the platoons quick reactions and decision-making when encountering the enemy. One of the tasks that the nighttime training required of my platoon was how to respond when we saw unexpected flares shot into the air. My platoon needed to find immediate cover from the light of the flares. Doing this would allow our platoon to remain on the trail without giving up our position on the ground. Finding cover from the flares in the sky hid our position from the enemy platoons. My platoon would remain out of sight until the flare had completely burned out and the only light in the nighttime sky was the moon. For our safety there were muzzles on our M-16s, and we also used blanks for bullets. The night war games were so much fun that we almost forgot that our lives could depend on this training.

Early, the next morning my platoon packed up all of our belongings and everything that we had brought to the field training back into our backpacks. My company got into platoon formation and was led back to the barracks at the sound of our drill sergeants voice commands and songs. Though I was happy to leave the field training, I really enjoyed the experience itself and the skills I obtained from it. While marching back to the barracks all I could think about was a hot shower, because after two weeks in the bush every one smelled liked pig knuckles and corn chips. When I saw the barracks from the distance the platoons started to chant the marching song that the drill sergeants orchestrated a little louder. The barracks seemed like an elaborate king's palace after two weeks in the field. My platoon had only that evening to relax, because at the crack of dawn our rigorous basic training schedule was set to resume.

The Bravo Company had no female recruits training with us. The only time we saw the other sex was at Sunday morning church services. The church on Fort McClellan accepted all Christian denominations, and did not discriminate against any other religion. On Sunday's the church was always standing room only. The church services and the unannounced visits to the barracks on our down time were the only breaks recruits got from basic training and the drill sergeants. The house of the

Lord was a way for some recruits to be around women, to pass letters to one another, and to forge new friendships.

The last task that I completed in basic training was the 25-mile road march through the hills of Fort McClellan. The march started long before the sun ever thought about coming up, and was finished by early morning. The 25-mile road march tested our stamina, determination, and physical strength to never quit no matter what obstacle was set before us. The march also separated the boys from the men and the recruits from the soldiers. During the march there were checkpoints in place for us to re-hydrate and exchange our wet socks for dry ones. The dry socks prevented our feet from injury or irritation due to rubbing against our leather boots. Those recruits who did not make the 25-mile march were recycled to another recruitment class, which meant they had to repeat basic training. Some recruits were recycled if they did not pass all required test. My bunk buddy got recycled when he did not pass the rifle range after several tries. Other recruits who want no parts of the training found other ways to get discharged. A few recruits forced the drill sergeants to submit the paper work for them to be kicked out of the Army.

Every recruit that remained in my platoon thought graduation day would never come, but when it did, we wore spiffy green class A's with shiny brass belt buckles. This would be the last time our platoon would be together, because after graduation most of us were going to different posts for Advanced Individual Training (AIT) somewhere in the States. So, as our company commander called Bravo Company to attention for the last time all platoons sounded off louder than they ever shouted during basic training. As companies marched around the parade field and gave their last salutes to the post commander, I felt like life's pressures had loosened their grip on me, and I was headed in the right direction. Graduation day was also a reflection of the hard work and dedication every recruit had put into becoming a **"United States Army Soldier"**.

Once, the basic training graduation ceremony ended all the platoons that were in Bravo Company returned to the barracks for a brief celebration with family members that came to support a watch their soldier graduate. Some of us had a couple of hours to visit with family members. The soldiers (like me) whose families did not attend the graduation, said their final goodbyes to everyone in the platoon. Gathered all of our belongings and stuff most of them in our large Army green duffle bags and back packs. We then loaded up on the big bright yellow school buses that had been idling in the parking lot since the basic training graduation ceremony. Once we were all loaded on the school buses, the school buses then transported us on a two hours ride on I-20 to Hartsfield-Jackson Atlanta International Airport. Our flight arrangements had already been made by Army personnel and each of us had copies of our orders with instructions on where to catch our flights to our next duty station. The next duty station that I was going to was Advanced Individual Training (AIT), which was specified training for the job I had chosen when I was sworn in at San Antonio, Texas. The training was mostly hands on training in the field with little classroom learning. The Army always trains new recruits for infantry assignments first, and then the recruits' military occupation second.

November 1991, I landed at the Newport News Williamsburg International Airport and was greeted by a driver bearing a sign that said Fort Eustis standing by a white government van. Once again I was traveling in the wee hours of the morning and woke up to the driver screaming that this was the last stop and everyone needs to get out of his van. I jumped up and grabbed my gear while still half sleep stumbled out of the van and onto the black top parking lot at Echo Company. Once the warm reception we received from Echo Company drill sergeants was over, they happily reminded us that first formation was at 5:00 a.m. which meant we only had two hours to sleep before I started my second phase of training, which was AIT as an 88H Cargo Specialist. The drill sergeants in AIT had the same attitude and intensity as the basic training drill sergeants, but I noticed that the AIT drill sergeants genuinely wanted each soldier to graduate from AIT.

My days in AIT were still long, but after the specialized training during the day, we were allowed to take the rest of the evening off. Some of us relaxed and watched TV, and other's got their uniform and equipment ready for the next day. AIT was also the first opportunity for some of us to mingle with opposite sex without supervision from drill sergeants. The female recruits were housed in the same barracks as their male counterparts. However, the female section of the barracks was always off limits to male recruits. Most of the male and female interaction happened in the TV room or away from the barracks. AIT allowed some soldiers to leave on weekend passes, but the weekend pass had to be earned during the week. Most of the soldiers who received a weekend pass went to the Patrick Henry mall to shop, to restaurants, and to the movies all in the same area. Many of the soldiers on a weekend pass stay in hotel rooms for a weekend of pampering from the hotel staff. Rather than coming back to the nagging drill sergeants that supervised the remaining soldiers cleaning the barracks and other activities. There was a great deal of sexual stress being released from all soldiers after being restrained for two months in basic training. Those who did not earn weekend passes had to stay around the barracks and had a curfew. Some soldiers disregarded the no sex rule and were caught by drill sergeants having sex in and around the barracks.

I met a young lady named Trisha from Memphis, Tennessee who was very pretty and smart. Trisha was still a virgin at the time, and seemed to have a quiet personality, which was usually for a person growing up in Memphis. Nothing became of the relationship, because when we graduated from AIT our new duty stations were in different states. We tried to have a long distance relationship, but the distance kept our hearts apart and there was no quality time spent, just long distance phone conversations.

Graduation from AIT was not as grand as my basic training graduation; still it played a significant role in proving to me and to the Army that this was where I belonged. I had the misfortune of being stationed at Fort Eustis, Virginia where I also spent my AIT training. I really felt like I had been robbed of the opportunity to travel around the States and duty stations in other countries. At this point I believed that all of the advertising and promoting commercials about all of the benefits of the joining the Army were just propaganda to get people to sign their young life away.

After the AIT graduation I had only a couple of hours to pack all my belonging and get out of the barracks. I had to carry all of my belongings to the welcome center at Fort Eustis. I then showed my orders to the clerk and the clerk noticed that I was assigned to 567th Transportation Company. The 567th TC had the reputation of being the worst and the roughest company on post. 567th TC was well known by the military police, because it seemed like the MP's were at 567th barracks every weekend. The first day of my arrival at 567th the MP's were chasing a soldier on a high performance motorcycle that was registered to a soldier in the 567th. The MP's could not compete with the speed of the motorcycle, or the skill of the soldier.

567th TC was a company that had soldiers from all walks of life; most of the soldiers were young adults. The older soldiers that had been in the company for a while were the soldiers to turn to when you got into certain situations. The barracks housed a majority of the single soldiers in the company and soldiers that were married, but temporarily separated from their spouses.

During my first weekend at 567th T.C. I met Specialist (SPC) Newberry, who had been in the company for a while and he instantly took me under his wing. That Friday night we rolled out to a nightclub that had Naughty by Nature in the house. This was when Naughty by Nature had their hit song out, "You down with OPP".

I reluctantly told SPC Newberry that I was not old enough yet to get into a 21 and older nightclub, at the time I was only 19 years old. SPC Newberry started laughing and told me not to worry about my age, just be ready to get girls phone numbers. I said "Cool," as he turned his radio back up. When we arrived at the nightclub, there was a long line wrapped around the building, but SPC Newberry had been to this nightclub before and knew how to get us in ahead of the crowd. As we cut through the line and made our way to the front door of the nightclub, SPC Newberry started politicking with one of the bouncers, when a fight broke out in the parking lot of the nightclub. So the bouncers left the front door to help with the fight and we easily paid our admission and entered the building. This was my first time in a nightclub of this magnitude and I was amazed at all the pretty women. Virginia really lives up to the state motto of "Virginia is for lovers." Even though I did not get to meet Naughty by Nature they seemed to be some really cool brothers. At this point in my life I was not a frequent drinker of alcohol and whatever I did drink would get me drunk pretty quickly. I was standing close to the dance floor and had a little buzz from the beer that SPC Newberry bought me from the bar. All of a sudden I noticed a pretty looking female coming towards me. As I attempted to grab her arm she turned to faced me.

I asked her, "Do you want to dance?" She smiled and laughed, when she noticed half closed eyes, and the effect the beer had on me. The beer bottle was still almost full, but expression showed that I was buzzing. We danced the entire night and I got those digits but never called.

SPC Newberry and I left the nightclub before it closed and headed back to Fort Eustis. I fell asleep in the car, but as we pulled up to the Fort Eustis entrance and the Military Police checkpoint he woke me up, because he did not want to give the MP's at the check point any reason to pull us to the side and administer a sobriety test. Most of the time on returning to post soldiers would allow the person who supposedly drank the least took the driver's seat before they reached the post MP checkpoint.

The next weekend I went out with fellow group of soldiers who lived on the same floor as I did in the barracks. That weekend of partying in Portsmouth, VA opened my eyes and exposed me something I had never before experienced. On the way home from the nightclub we were so drunk and tired that the driver of the car pulled off the highway onto the access road and fell asleep with everyone else in the car. We slept on the access road into the early morning, until somebody woke up and started yelling for all of us to wake up. Once we all were awake it was hard to believe that we all fell asleep on the side of the road. "Thank you God for watching over us." When everyone checked out to be okay, we then started laughing and making jokes about how we ended up on the side of the road asleep. Once we got back to Fort Eustis in Newport News, VA or (Bad News) we stopped at a local eatery for breakfast and swore not to tell anyone what happened to us once we got back to the barracks.

The soldiers who lived in the barracks took pride in what floor they lived on. There were always competitions going on like what room stayed the cleanest and organized. The waxing of the hallway was the most important competition and soldiers took great pride in waxing their portion of the hallway. There were always mandatory Sunday meetings in the barracks to make sure all the soldiers who lived in the barracks showed up and participated.

567th TC was not as bad as everyone I had talked to made the company out to be. After being in 567th TC for a couple of years everyone treated each other like we were one big family. It took a special person and soldier to be in the 567th TC. 567th and the 24th battalion won the majority of competitions that took place around the base. Our battalion football team had an undefeated season and had bragging rights around the base. Other companies accused the 567th TC of being arrogant. Yes we were arrogant and always had a certain swagger to our walk and marching because we knew that we were the best. Many people who talked down on the 567th were just jealous and envious of the 567th Airborne "D". Unfortunately, whenever there was a deployment sent down the chain of command the first company selected was the 567th T.C.

I got my first taste of deployment on January 4, 1993, when my platoon from the 567th TC was selected to deploy with the 119th TC, because the company needed additional soldiers to complete the mission in Mogadishu, Somalia. The first night in theatre my platoon slept in the field right off the runway strip. During the night I could sometimes feel the heat from the aircraft engines as they took off down the runway. Where we slept was of no concern to me, because I had been on a 22-hour flight from Langley Air Force Base to Africa and had very little sleep during the flight. I was more excited than scared to experience my first deployment. I was also excited to be going back to the motherland -- the birthplace of my ancestor's. Once brass found out where my platoon was staying, we were then put into groups of four and waited for the black hawk helicopters to pick us up and deposit us at the drop point. From the drop point my platoon, with all of our gear attached, marched to the Mogadishu port.

The mission was called Restore Hope and the army's primary goal was to stop the warlords in the country from cutting off food supplies to their own people, causing a pre-emptive mass genocide by starvation. "A dictator can only remain in power as long as the people he governs remain divided, fearful, and ignorant." The mission seemed somewhat successful from what I had witnessed. Being a driver for the commander allowed me to see much of the country side and I noticed that the longer the military presence was in theater, the more Somalian people trusted us. The Somalian warlords had scaled down some of their attacks on the United Nations, and were more reluctant to initiate more dangerous isolated incidents.

The most notorious and world-recognized incident was the "Black Hawk Down" disaster. Once we located the warehouse was located where we would be housed for the next four-months, we then unpacked our duffle bags and set up our sleeping quarters. Africa felt like I had been here before in another life. To me it really felt like I had come back home.

RECRUIT 2 ARMY SOLDIER

The days were hot, but because we lived on the Mogadishu port there was always a cool breeze at night.

Mogadishu was our new home, so we had to build our own amenities, such as showers, mess hall, and latrines. Because I was the lowest ranked in my squad, I got stuck with the latrines duties. My job was to take the filled barrels of feces and urine from under the toilet seat in the latrines, and then carry the filled barrels to the empty location, which was a deep trench that had been dug into the ground. Afterward, someone would pour a flammable chemical onto the waste and then light the cocktail. We waited at the trench and watched the burning waste form a black cloud, which ultimately evaporated into the air. I cannot begin to explain how terrible the waste smelled, from the bowels of more than a couple thousand troops marinating in the hot sun.

Fortunately, I got promoted from the latrine job to a guard on convoys to the embassy in the city of Mogadishu. I never considered the danger of our mission. I just loved going full speed through the city until we got to the embassy. We had been briefed that if we slowed down or had to make an unauthorized stop our vehicle might be over taken by renegade Somalians.

There was an event I recall that happened one night about two months into my tour in Somalia. This night was no different from any other spent in the warehouse on the port. However, around midnight, as most of my platoon slumbered, a loud boom exploded in the rear of our lodging, which shook the warehouse and woke everyone up. Then there was another boom, which sounded like a mortar round. Everyone in the warehouse panicked. Some of the men jumped straight up off their cots, taking their mosquito nets with them, and ran for cover. The alarm blared and soldiers rushed to get to their designated meeting spot. A few marine companies occupied the warehouse with us; and all I heard from their side was the loading and locking of their weapons. After a few hours the alert was called off and we returned to the warehouse.

The night shift was cool to work, but during the day sleep was impossible due to the heat and constant commotion of trucks loading and unloading on the pier. There was also constant hammering and other construction work being done on the roof of the warehouse and around it. There were many rainy days and nights, which seemed to bring a temporary quiet and peace to this barren part of Africa.

On April 9, 1993, I returned to Fort Eustis, Virginia from Mogadishu, Somalia, where I had spent four months on a humanitarian mission. The Army made a huge impact on my life and many of the lessons learned while serving allowed me to become a well-respected citizen and a more mature man. It was in the Army that I discovered how to respect authority and later how to use authority, where necessary, in civilian life.

In the years that followed my first deployment to Africa, and my return to Fort Eustis, Virginia, I made big detours in the life I had planned for myself. While in Africa I had the opportunity to see the lack of things that most American's take for granted, such as easy access to running water; taking a shower; eating a hot meal; or having the right to do whatever you want to do -- within reason. Freedom of speech or just having a opinion when we disagree with our leaders and government, is a right in the United States. I realized that it is quite different elsewhere in the world, where imprisonment can result from merely voicing an opposing view than is held by a dictator of one's country.

However, before I would allow any positive metamorphosis to take place, I strayed away from the destiny that my GOD had planned for my life. Once back in Fort Eustis I hooked up with my fellow soldiers, and we indulged ourselves in much partying, sex, alcohol, lying, and player behavior. It was somewhat of an honor in the barracks to be a player, where most of the single male soldiers lived and competed, as we purposely sought to see who could juggle the most women without getting caught up.

Because of this contest there was always drama in the barracks, which could easily have become a hit reality show. I had adapted at this point the mentality of a person who cared not if I lived or died. I can truly say that I did not love myself and did not care about the consequences of my actions. Waking up drunk from partying all night was not a good feeling, but it was a kind of insane therapy that I used to free myself from facing my troubled life.

By late summer of 1993 I had strayed so far from the Lord that I even questioned how powerful GOD is. On a hot summer's day, my fellow soldiers and I decided to have a cookout in the courtyard in the rear of the barracks. Everyone pitched in to buy the supplies and food. The cookout was a success and we had a wonderful time. We felt good, thanks to all of the joy juice consumed after we ate our food. I had a little too much to drink and was feeling a little tipsy. I had never been the type of person, who drank alcohol every day, but when I did drink at clubs or social events I would always drink more than I could handle. My fellow soldiers put pressure on me to drink, because they knew that I was generally a light weight. Once fully intoxicated I would then tell all of them how really felt about them.

One day I received a call from a girl named Angela whom I had met at the PX (Post Exchange) earlier that week. Angela actually worked at the PX and several of the male soldiers on the base had been trying to get her number. This would be a huge notch on my belt if Angela came to the cookout looking for me. So, I gave her directions to where I was on the base. Angela promised that she would come to see me when she got off work.

A couple of hours passed before Angela showed up looking fly as ever. The jealousy and envy emanating from the soldiers was evident by their expressions, when they found out that I was the man she was looking for. I tried my damndest to hide from Angela the fact that I had consumed one too many alcoholic drinks by holding my drunkenness to a minimum. Of course, she could smell the alcohol and see my valentine red eyes. Thankfully, I was not too intoxicated to leave the cookout with her and go to the local mall. Before we left, however, I requested that she drive, using the excuse that my car was out of gas. She agreed, but it was clear that she recognized that I was in no condition to drive anything, let alone a car. The longer I was with her, the soberer I became.

During the drive back to Fort Eustis from the mall, I told Angela that I had noticed her in the PX, but never said anything because I assumed that she had a boyfriend. Angela stated that a lot of the soldiers that come to the PX think that, and for that reason they never ask her out on date.

I responded "I'm glad they think that, because now you do have a boyfriend." She got a big laugh out of that one, which made her really smile and show a happy side of her that I had not seen during our trip to the mall.

Once we drove into the parking lot of my barracks, I asked "Would you like to come up to my room for a while?" I was surprised when she smiled, and said "Yes," I knew the guys in the barracks were going to have salty looks when we walked into the barracks, and particularly when Angela went to my room.

RECRUIT 2 ARMY SOLDIER

"Hey, Haywood," someone yelled from across the street, "I need to talk to you." Angela and I stopped at the steps leading to my barracks; I looked at Angela. "Be right back," I said. As I turned to respond to the person calling me from the other side of the street, Angela said faintly "They sound like they want to fight you." I turned and gave her a Kool-Ade smile and continued walking toward the person who had summoned me. I knew his face, because our companies had served together in Somalia. I laughed inside, because I thought he planned to tell me something or ask a favor. As I proceeded, I noticed that the guys he was sitting with rose from the bench and began walking towards me. Soon I was surrounded by a crowd. As I squared up with the face I knew, I saw two of his boys getting ready to hit me from the blind spot. I attempted to get out of the crowd and that's when someone tripped me and I fell to the ground. I covered myself up (HOW?), so that the three of them did not do any physical damage. Only my pride was hurt a little. Spc. Ponder helped me up off the ground. Ponder was an older soldier in my company, but everyone on base respected him. Spc. Ponder told me to go to the barracks and not try to fight the three soldiers. Once off the ground I started cursing -- calling them bitches, and told them that this fight was not over. Once the soldiers in my company found out what had happen to me, they first did not believe it. But once they were convinced of the truth, they asked me what I wanted to do. They were ready for war, and pulled out the guns they had stashed away for such times as this. I told them that the punks that jumped me did not hurt me and that I would handle the matter myself. Spc. Williams pulled me to the side and gave me his loaded 45 handgun. The craziest soldier in my company, Spc. Williams was treated like the big brother of the barracks. I gladly took the 45 handgun and started to plot my revenge, which would have to be a sneak attack, because if I did something now everyone would know that I was the guilty party. I wanted to do the crime and not the time in a federal prison.

After the word got around the base that I had got supposedly beat down by the three punks, everyone came to check on me. One female soldier that I knew from another company on the base was with the punks who jumped me. Spc. Dee informed me that she had advised them not to hit me in the face, because I was a pretty boy. She had come to check on me to see how my face was. Listening to Spec. Dee's statement to my assailants made me laugh and brought me back to reality.

Someone must have been praying for me, because a couple of days after the fight I was going to take out my first target. I did not keep the 45 hand gun on base, because living in the barracks soldiers are subjected to searches at any time and private hand guns needed to be locked up in the arms room, as they were prohibited on base. If a soldier is caught with an unregistered hand gun on or off base that soldier would be immediately processed out of the service with a dishonorable discharge. I kept the 45 hand gun off base at a friend's house. After retrieving the 45 I was ready to execute the first part of my revenge plan, at which time I drove to the place where I suspected the first guy would be. My strategy was to approach and shoot him. I wanted him to see my face as I pulled the trigger.

When I got about a mile from my destination, I was stopped by a Virginia state trooper. I removed the 45 hand gun from the passenger seat and put it in my inner coat pocket. If the trooper asked me to step out of the car, I would have to go to plan B, and that did not include going to jail. After the trooper asked for my driver's license and registration, a calming voice spoke into my ear, advising me to stay calm. The trooper returned to my car, gave me back my driver's license and registration, and said "Have a nice day."

I only received a warning for speeding and was told to "slow it down." Sometimes I still wonder what turn my life would have taken had not that cop asked me to step out of the car. While in deep thought a voice inquired, "Are these dudes worth killing and going to jail for the rest of my life." I know the Lord was intervening when he sent the state trooper to stop me. Once I reached the guy, I just rolled past him and when he saw my car, a look of fear suffused his face, as though his spirit was pleading for his life. His expression alerted me that he was not worth killing and I did not have to worry about him anymore.

Guy two I caught at the gas station with his girl and he ran like a little bitch. Some of the soldiers in my company told me that they caught the guys who had jumped me at different places and served them up real nice. Nobody on GOD's green earth messes with any soldier from the 567th TC (Airborne D).

On February 9, 1997 my life flashed before my eyes, while sitting at a red light. I was abruptly struck from behind by a vehicle going about 60 mph. The impact made my head hit the front windshield, even though I had my seat belt on. Had I not had my seat belt on the impact would surely have thrown me from the car. The person who hit me had to be cut out of his car and rushed to the hospital for treatment. For some unknown reason my flight or fight response kicked in and I left the scene of the accident. Because I left the scene I was deemed to be at fault, and was subsequently charged with a hit and run.

In the following months I had to appear in court, but first I had to find a lawyer who would take my case. My first attorney did a lousy job of representing me, so I fired him and retained a local lawyer, who was brilliant in pinpointing my first lawyer's mistakes, which resulted in my charges being reduced to reckless driving. I was happy to get the case behind me, inasmuch as during the court drama I was also processing out of the Army. Fortunately, I was able to keep the Army out of my personal life, because a court case of this magnitude would have caused me to receive a dishonorable discharge. Thank you GOD for watching over me, and making August 22, 1997 successful on two fronts: my honorable discharge from the Army and my final court appearance to fight the hit and run charge. Of course, I still had to pay restitution to the person that hit me from behind with a blood alcohol level three times higher than the legal limit. I once again thank GOD for intervening and bringing me out of a tight situation.

9

Test of Faith

On September 1997 I enrolled at Hampton University, eager to start the next chapter of my life and close the old chapter. Just being on the HU campus made me feel that anything was possible; I just had to go and get it. Registering for my classes was an all day event, because as soon as I moved from one registration line the next one was that much longer. I already had taken some college courses and knew that my major would be in accounting, because I enjoyed working with numbers. Accounting has so many different professional employment fields a student can chose from once they graduate. After paying course fees, I went to the book store and bought all my books. I then headed home to Newport News, VA, where I stayed in a townhouse with some guys I knew in the military. In the beginning the living arrangements worked out great, but all good things come to an end. The person in charge of collecting rent and utility money from all the roommates did not pay the bills as they were due. Instead this person would pay only the minimum on the bills and the extra money left over went into his pocket. I also did not like the fact that when his friends would visit from out of town they would stay with us, keeping the townhouse crowded all the time. When I came home late at night after being in classes all day and studying in the library, someone was usually asleep in my bed. I put up with this as long as I could, but one weekend when I got off my work I was finally fed up.

On a warm Sunday afternoon I was cruising around the city of Hampton in my burnt orange Mitsubishi Eclipse, while looking for a cheap apartment to rent. My fuel was getting low, so I pulled into a gas station and there she was -- my future Queen. As I drove around to where she was pumping gas, my car caught her attention. I got out, approached her and politely asked if she wanted me to pump her gas. She declined with a smile, implying that I had a small window of opportunity and that she was not falling for the common hook and reel in lines. I told her my name and asked if she would do me the honor of giving me hers. "Samantha," she said.

Samantha had just moved to the Hampton area and was staying with her cousin. We talked about ten minutes more before I asked if I could call her sometimes and she said, "Yes."

On my way home to Bad News, Samantha was on my mind real heavy. The one-day waiting period to call a female after getting her number went out the window. I called Samantha later that evening and we talked most of the night, agreeing to meet the next day for dinner. I felt that we had a true connection and she was also laughing at my corny jokes. Samantha was definitely the woman for me, at dinner she told me her situation and that she was looking for a place to rent. I told her that I lived in Bad News and the reason I was in the city of Hampton was to enroll at Hampton University and look for an apartment. After a few weeks of talking to Samantha, she found a place to rent and asked if I would move in with her

TEST OF FAITH

and her nine-year old daughter Sasha. Sasha was very smart for her age and we clicked the first time that we met. I agreed to move in because the duplex that Samantha rented was only five minutes away from the Hampton University campus. I later found out that Samantha was also a good cook, when she cooked some collard greens that were so good I could have slapped somebody. Those collard greens sealed the deal for me. As the old adage goes -- the way to a man heart is through his stomach, and mine was feeling full and good.

Samantha had a laid back attitude that complemented my laid back attitude so we really enjoyed being around each other. I do not remember any arguments during the two years that we dated. Samantha catered to all my needs,
dinner was always ready when I came home.

On the first day of class at Hampton University Samantha got up and cooked me breakfast and gave me a kiss for good luck. My classes at Hampton were great, but I was always the oldest in my classes, because Hampton University undergraduates were mostly composed of traditional college students. Everyone looked at me as the older brother who could buy alcohol. Hampton business school made students work hard and allowed most accounting majors to work as team members when needed. I had already mastered working as a team while serving six years in the U.S. Army.

The accounting majors took the majority of their classes together; they studied, and worked on class assignments together, helping each other when needed. During my last semester at Hampton I was part of a team that created a Business Seminar Course. The BSC included all business school students; we solicited fortune 500 companies to visit Hampton University for the purpose of hiring business school students. During the seminars, the companies would be briefed on the school's history and in what direction the business school was headed. The information session also highlighted why Hampton Business School students were the best and only smart choice for their companies.

Hampton business classes kept me in the library a great deal and away from home. Concurrent with my studies, I founded and maintained an independent record label named DA FAM Records. I had one act that I tried to break into the music industry using my own unorthodox method of management.

I just hit the streets of
Bad News and Hampton roads looking for a way to get this group some exposure locally before we went to the radio and television circuit. The Realm of Darkness was a rap group with all members coming from the east coast. I knew the members several years before, when we both served in the Army at Fort Eustis and in the 567th Transportation Company.

The Hampton Roads area was filled with veterans who had been discharged from the military. In fact, Hampton Roads had all branches of the military services in that on small area. Most service members spent a great deal of their tour in the Hampton Roads vicinity, and naturally made Virginia their home when they got discharged from the service.

The Realm of Darkness was talented, so I decide to make them the debut act of DA FAM Records and to use the experience to gain exposure, while learning the business side of the entertainment industry. I had also just completed my third semester at Hampton University as an accounting student and had big plans for DA FAM records. So, I invested into the rap group, because I truly believed they had a good product, which would be mutually beneficial. We began appearing in local talent shows - and were ready to take our product to the next level. One of the members of the group had received news

TEST OF FAITH

from his cousin that he had already been signed by a major label, and wanted us to come to Philadelphia to meet him. The last time this group member had seen his cousin was when they were children, and they had not spoken since. The artist's name was Kasino, who resided in Yonkers, NY, but was in Philly to promote his new song and video. Kasino had done some previous collaboration with a another well-known group from Yonkers. Kasino turned out to be a real cool dude and told me if I needed anything to just call. I truly appreciated the love and his willingness to help us out. Kasino was different from other new artists, whose heads tend to swell, and they and forget from whence they came. Everything is about their little five minutes of fame.

The relationship between Samantha and I began to unravel, because I was in the street politicking, which resulted in less quality time spent with her. The only moments I spent with Samantha were when I was exhausted from the night before and slept most of the day. Samantha started making comments, which lead to her telling me that she was unhappy with our relationship. I blew it off, because I was banking on when the label started making money that she would understand my reason for being away so often. There was a very good reason why Samantha wanted me to be at home more, because she knew something that I did not.

In April 1998, Samantha told me that she was pregnant and wanted to have the baby. Initially, I did not know what to say, because my brain was trying to process the information. Of course, I knew she had said something about a baby. Once my brain confirmed her comment, I agreed and with a Kool-Ade smile, I responded that I wanted to have the baby, too. The pressure of having a baby and not being able to provide for it weighed heavy on my mind. So I put my hustling skills into overdrive and decided against taking any classes at Hampton University in the fall of 1999.

Samantha's pregnancy seemed to go quite well, I was trying my best to avoid putting any stress on her. I would ask if she wanted anything and when I was out I called home and asked, if she wanted me to bring her something from the store on the way home. Midway through Samantha's pregnancy she began spitting a great deal into cups, and stated the reason to be because "The baby is going to have a full head of hair." As the expected delivery date loomed closer and closer sleep became elusive. Excitement at the prospect of seeing my first creation was overwhelming.

On December 31, 1998 at 10:00 p.m, Samantha awakened me with the news that the baby was coming and we needed to get to the hospital. I bolted up, got dressed and rushed down the stairs to warm up the car. I then went back into the house to help Samantha downstairs and into the car. Snow was still on the ground from the heavy storm earlier in the day. I sped to the hospital, but with extreme caution. My heart was beating so fast I felt that it might jump out of my chest at any moment. As I pulled up to the guard station at Langley Air Force Base I showed I.D. and then proceeded to the hospital. I parked the car by the front emergency exit door and escorted Samantha into the emergency room. Samantha was greeted by the hospital staff and the nurse on duty asked her a couple of routine question, but the staff could clearly see that she was suffering from repeated contractions. While the staff placed Samantha in a wheel chair and steered her to the maternity ward, I hurried back outside to park the car in the lot. The car secured, I dashed through the hospital until I reached Samantha's room. She was still having contractions, but they were too far apart and her water had not yet broken. Samantha initially informed the nurses that she wanted to have the baby the natural way, but when the pains started coming more frequently she asked for an epidural.

After several hours the doctor decided to induce- labor, and on January 1, 1999 at 8:00 a.m. the most beautiful little baby girl was born into this crazy world. "Thank You GOD." The doctor gave me the shears to cut the umbilical cord, I did and my baby girl was officially here amongst us. How unbelievable that I had contributed to the creation of something so beautiful and pure! Miss TKH was the second baby born in Virginia that morning, so she did not receive all the attention and free stuff given to the first baby born into the New Year. I, for one, did not care because I was going to give my baby girl the world if it killed me. Samantha's cousin and her husband came to the hospital and told me to go home and get some sleep, but I could not sleep, as I was still in awe of our creation.

February 15, 1999 on an early Sunday morning I awoke and my girl friend Samantha told me that she wanted us to go and visit her friend's church. My youngest daughter was only a month and a half then. I was a very proud Dad and was eager to show off my baby girl. When we finally made it to the church after getting lost and with a low tank of gas we shouted hallelujah when we finally found the church. During the service I felt something come into my spirit and heard the Lord speak to me. The Lord told me that it was time for me to end my sinful life and follow him, so I immediately jumped out of my seat and ran to the alter where the pastor was and dedicated my life to the Lord. Samantha thought it strange that I would give my life to Christ in a church that I had only then set foot in. I did not even know the name of the church. Nonetheless, I did not hesitate or think twice; because when you know the Lord is telling you to do something you do it

– in that moment wherever you are. The repercussions of not doing the Lord's bidding could be death and your soul being eternally damned to hell. The Lord knows you before you are born into this world and the Lord sometimes permits the devil to test you to see how obedient you are and just how strong is your faith in Him. The reason the Lord spoke to me on this day was because He was preparing me for what would happen later that night. As I raised my hands and recited the words the pastor bade me, it were as if lightning bolts scintillated through my stomach. I felt as though all the evil spirits and demons that were inside me had rushed out of my body. This experience was scary, as I had never before experienced anything even remotely like it. "Glory Hallelujah." The preacher continued to pray for the new members and the people who wanted to rededicate their lives to Christ, and change their sinful ways. The congregants crowded around the altar for this uplifting ceremony. After the dedication of souls to Christ the assistant pastors asked us to follow them to a room they had set up for new believers and members. The room was full to overflowing with people. When church services were over the pastor walked into the room and asked us individually, "What is the reason you to want to live for Christ now?" When the pastor finally got to me I was very anxious to tell him about my experience at the podium. The pastor looked at me and smiled and in a subtle voice asked me, "Do you think it was the devil." I went blank after the last word that the pastor spoke to me and all I could remember was the word DEVIL. When I regained my composure I could not believe what the pastor had asked me. Before this day I had truly believed that I was in God's grace, and as long as I believed in Him, prayed at night, and repented I was safe from the devil. Little did I know that on this day God was going to let me decide to go to heaven or hell? I believe that

TEST OF FAITH

had I not chosen God, I would not be alive today sharing my testimony with the world. God was going to lift His hand off of me and allow the devil to destroy me. "The devil has to ask God's permission to mess with His people". Christians should always be in the word and stay prayed up, because you never know when you will be tested by the devil.

When I left the room and found Samantha and the girls, we gathered all our belongings and then left the church. During the ride home it was so quiet in the car as to be slightly uncomfortable. I did not mention what had taken place at the church with pastor. I - remained quiet until we reached home. The church service made me think about my family and my days of running the streets. I now knew that I had to change my life and make GOD the number one priority.

As I laid on the couch in the living room, I was still recovering from a cold that I had caught on Friday. When the cold medicine kicked in I suddenly fell into a deep sleep.

February 16, 1999 at 1:00 a.m. I awoke from my long nap not feeling well. My mind was racing and something was talking to me as though it were taking over my spirit. The heavy rain beat on the windows like a drum line. I was used to rainy nights in Virginia, because it rained quite often during the winter months. When I finally got out bed I went and took a hot shower. Meanwhile it was lighting and thundering outside. When I got out of the shower my life changed for the worse.

3:45 a.m. I was watching religious infomercials that came on in the wee hours of the morning on BET, which is when I snapped. I woke Samantha up and told her, she needed to get saved. Samantha looked at me and asked, "What in the hell is wrong with you, do you know what time it is?" We then started to argue, because she did not like me waking her up, telling her that she needed to get saved. Our voices started to get louder the more Samantha saw that I was serious about what I said. Before this point in our relationship Samantha and I had never had any serious arguments. Starting an argument with her was not normal for me. As the argument escalated Samantha and I left our bedroom and proceeded down the stairs to the living room.

Half way down the stairs I shouted "I will kill you if you don't get saved." Samantha was only 4"11" and about 5ft on a good day. I was then 6"3" 220 and had gained some weight since I was discharged from the military. Samantha's good cooking was also part of the reason for the weight gained. She was fattening me up. When she heard, "I Will Kill You," and saw the expression on my face, Samantha ran out the front door and went to a neighbor's house to call the police. It was like I had turned into a black incredible HULK. I then fell to my knees butterball naked and started praying, because I felt like my mind was gone and that someone else were at the controls.

A few minutes passed, after which something spoke to me and told me to call the police and tell the operator that I had just killed my wife. During my conversation with the 911 operator, I learned that the police were already in route. My oldest daughter and my newborn daughter were in the bed sleeping. My oldest daughter woke up when she heard the screaming voices, but remained in her room.

There was a soft knock at the door, so I got off my knees and proceeded to unlock and open the front door; I thought Samantha had come back home, once she had HAD time to regroup. As I unlocked the door it swung open to reveal four police officers ready for battle. They rushed in with their baton's swinging and after a short struggle and me receiving a Rodney King ass whipping, I was handcuffed and put in a police car. I had no idea what was going on, as I had never felt nor acted this way before in my entire life. On my way to jail in the cramped back seat of the police car I had to sit in the car sideways, because the police always push their seats all the way back. So when arrested, patrons have no room for their legs and feet. I started preaching the word of GOD to the police officer driving me to jail and got him saved. The officer initially thought that I was using illegal drugs and had just got some of that uwwe uuuh from the dope man. Once at the jail I was placed alone in a cell. After close observation, the police decided something was wrong and called in a nurse to make a determination of what was going on with me. Was I just high, or was I mentally ill after all the commotion I started to feel that the Lord was angry with me. Because of my disobedience and detour from the righteous path, the Lord had called my number. The Lord then came to me while I was still in my jail cell and asked me if I wanted 2 Live or Die and I replied I wanted to Live for my newborn daughter and did not want to die. After several hours of observation the nurse then came back to my cell and tried to have a conversation with me, but I was unresponsive. That morning I was transported to Riverside hospital, put in a room and strapped to the bed. After a short span, my mind started to wonder again and bombs, machine guns, and mortar rounds went off inside my head. In a few hours, I began a slow return to reality, but had exerted myself into exhaustion and could not walk. The hospital staff came in, put me in a wheel chair and took me to the mental ward, where I was given a private room with a bed. I was almost too weak to move or stand. When the wheel chair got near my bed I had just enough strength to stand up and immediately collapsed onto the bed. I faintly remember that a nurse would ever so often awaken me to take medicine.

LIVING 2 DIE OR DYING 2 LIVE

The devil would have destroyed me, if the Lord had not spoken to me in church the previous day and allowed me to choose to follow him. God had given me another chance to continue living on this earth. I was released from the hospital later that day.

Back at home I felt that Samantha and my parents were walking on eggshells around me. Samantha had sent for my parents, because she was scared and did not know what was wrong with me. My mother had scared Samantha even more, by telling her that the people I was hanging around with had probably spiked my drink. The negative atmosphere that my mother brought to the house made matters worse. My mother never did have anything good to say about me during discussions with family members or other people. I guess Samantha believed most of it since it was coming from my mother, unaware that my mother would make you believe the sky was falling if you let her.

After my parents left Virginia and returned to Texas my relationship with Samantha fell apart and the atmosphere around the house was like we were walking around on pins and needles.

10

Finding GOD Again

After my psychotic episode, I knew that my relationship with Samantha - would never be the same. I had shown her a side of me that neither she nor I had ever seen before; I had never experienced anything like it and surely did not have a family history of mental illness.

When I was a young boy there were certain people in our neighborhood that my friends and I would name as "can't get right" person or a person who "was not all there upstairs". I was oblivious to the fact that mental illness affected millions of people -- some early in life and some as a young adult. I just thought that after all of the bad karma I had put out over the years it was finally my time to pay the piper. I had no clue what was going on with me, but I was desperately trying to shake off whatever had me in its iron grip. At this point I knew that my unexplained outburst and frequent displays of anger outside our house may have been funny to the neighbors, but they truly and totally embarrassed me and my family. The police were called to our house so often that one officer gave me his private number and told me to call him instead of calling 911.

LIVING 2 DIE OR DYING 2 LIVE

Every chance that I got that my ex-girlfriend allowed me to spend time with my little baby girl. I did. Her light brown eyes made me forget about my current situation. I had something to live for and protect from this crazy world. I would have to be strong and tighten up my boot straps because it was not all about me anymore. God had given me a gift that would love me unconditionally. Such a special love from my little daughter gave me the motivation and the strength to combat this storm.

Samantha insisted that I leave the house immediately after several arguments and the police being call and me being taken away in hand cuffs and after a month or so I gave in. I left the household in order to create a safer and quieter place for my children. There was no denying that it was time for me to leave, since Samantha and I whenever we came in contact with each other. So I packed what I could carry in my blue tub and headed towards the nearest bus stop. I rode the bus into downtown Newport News, VA and walked to the boarding house where I stayed after being released from the hospital following my second episode. I resided in the Hampton Roads area to be close to my daughters. I wanted to remain a part of their lives, and did I not want any other man raising my girls. After all, I had grown up in a house with a step-parent and was mistreated; I did not want the same fate for my daughter.

The boarding house was set up for men from all walks of life. Some residents were recovering from drug use, and had been kicked out - by their spouses and told the only way that they would be allowed to come back home was if they stopped using drugs. Some of the stories the men told were quite funny. Most of which revolved around the extremes to which they went in order to get a fix. We laughed for hours. The story I remember most was told by Ralph, who was a city transit bus driver. The story began one late night when Ralph was on his city bus route. He had cashed his check earlier that day and had an entire two weeks pay burning in his pocket. Ralph had been fighting temptation all day, because he knew that he could not have a relapse with his mortgage payment past due. The demons inside his head had convinced him that he could make a quick stop and only get a 20 rock for the ride home. That did not happen, as Ralph's addiction refused to let him wait until his tour ended. So, he took the bus off route and steered it to a vacant house in the trap. Ralph said he was probably in the trap for an hour or more but was not sure because he was getting higher than a kite. He did monitor the radio on the bus; and after several attempts by the dispatcher to locate Ralph, the police were alerted and the GPS system was activated. According to Ralph he finally roused himself, re-boarded the bus and pulled out of the driveway of the vacant house, at which time he was surrounded by the boys in blue. Ralph said he tried to explain to the police that he must have taken a wrong turn somewhere and got lost. However, the police did not believe him and took him into custody. Ralph was fired by the city before the police had clamped on the handcuffs. We laughed about Ralph's story until our stomachs hurt and tears formed in our eyes. I really enjoyed hearing the stories of how the men reached this point in life.

Some residents were in transition and had fulltime jobs at the boarding house thrift store, so that they could pay their weekly bed fee. The one good thing about living there is that they served breakfast and dinner, which allowed some of us to save the money that, would have been spent on food. What I did not like about the boarding house was the evening curfew; if you did not make curfew the door would be locked and you would have to spend the night outside and miss the mandatory bed check. After three missed bed checks with no explanation, all of your belongings were put into a plastic bag and your bed stripped. Upon returning to check in the next morning there was a flag by your name and you would not be allowed to enter the house. As if that weren't enough you would then have to wait outside on the steps for someone to bring your plastic bag out to you. The facility reopened its doors at around 6:00 a.m.; only then were you allowed to come in, take a shower and eat breakfast. After breakfast a couple of hours were allotted to make your bed and secure your belongings in a wall locker next to your bed. Anything left out was supposedly thrown away by the cleaning crew. All boarders had to vacate the house for the day and return in the evening at 5:00 p.m. when the doors reopened and dinner was served.

 I was homeless, but I did not let that affect my determination to overcome being homeless. On Sunday's I continued attending the church that Samantha and I frequented when we were still together. This was also the church where my baby girl was christened, so it held for me some sentimental value. On one Sunday afternoon I showed up for service wearing sweat pants and flip flops. This is what I felt comfortable in, and in any case, most of my clothing was still at Samantha's house. I really made good use of the saying -- "Come as you are to worship the Lord." The congregation did not treat me any different; they still showed me love. At the end of the service I went to the altar for prayer, the pastor actually hugged me instead of just shaking my hand and told me that everything was going to be okay. Thank you GOD for this anointed man of GOD.

 After all my big dreams and hopes for a successful future, I found myself walking amongst the less fortunate and the forgotten in society. People do not realize how close they are to being on the street and homeless. I also noticed when I was homeless and had that homeless look that people with whom I came in contact began treating me with disdain. People are funny, because they always preach and teach about helping each other but rarely do so. My situation reminded me of a song that my sister used to sing in church during the times that we went to church as a family and that song was "As long as I got King Jesus I Do Not Need Nobody Else."

The people I thought were my friends really were not. However, when I had money I had lots of friends. I am of the belief that if someone is in need, I will offer them my last dollar. When I was in the streets and going out to clubs Wednesday thru Sunday I would always foot the bill for everyone in my entourage. When my money ran out these same individuals ceased answering my phone calls. It hurt me very much at first, because I would have done anything for anybody if I could. I have always believed that everything happens for a reason and that in time GOD will make your enemies your footstool.

When I walked the streets during the day and night most people refused to acknowledge my presence. The public library is a popular place for homeless people; it was where I hung out during the day. I was still too messed up to look for or even hold a job. Some library staff members identified and closely monitored their homeless patrons, and showed little respect when we congregated there. The few library staff that participated in this kind of = monitoring truly made one feel worthless and as if you chose to be homeless and a strain on society. To avoid most of the yelling confrontations with library staff some of the homeless people just casually stood in huddles outside of the library. What type of society are we?

Being on the other side of the fence really showed me the true character of most people; I could count on one hand the people who genuinely showed that they cared about the homeless. Even, though I was homeless and wandering the streets of Bad News night and day, I did not let it get to me and did not let homelessness interfere with my responsibilities toward my baby girls. I continued to visit Samantha's house and pick my new born baby girl up, even though Samantha and I were having problems. After several weeks away from the house, Samantha allowed me to come back and I promised her that I was going to make everything all right. I was still suffering from my unexplained episodes and thought if I just stayed busy doing something that whatever condition I had would eventually go away. But without the proper treatment I was just a time bomb ticking until I exploded again. A few more weeks had passed when I once more began to lose touch with reality; the medicine that was prescribed for me had stop working and my aggressive outbursts became more frequent when things did not go my way. I really tried hard to put a lid on the outbursts because I knew this was the only way that I could keep peace in the house and keep my family together. A few months more had passed and I was looking for a job to help support the family.

While I searched the employment pages of the daily newspaper, I noticed that the jobs I qualified for did not pay very much. I needed to find a position that I could start immediately, with unlimited salary potential. I applied mostly at car dealerships for car salesman positions, which offered the opportunity for advancement. I knew that I was a good people person and people buy cars every day. The car salesman job would be my new hustle until I found something better. A few days had passed since I had applied at a huge Toyota dealership in Chesapeake, VA. I was encouraged when the manager of the sales department called me and scheduled an interview.

The next day I arrived for the interview well dressed and more than prepared to sell my skills and team attitude to the panel of interviewers. The waiting room was filled to capacity with potential new salespersons. I was one of the few they hired on the spot and started pre-training that day. During the first week I learned a lot about the workings of the dealership, as well as about the games that they play with customers. Used car dealerships make more money on the cars that they sell because the dealership can mark up their inventory above blue book value.

Sadly, the car salesman job did not work out like I had planned. One day during the salespersons training, I was called out of the classroom and told by one of the managers that they had to terminate my employment because of too many moving violations on my driving record. I was crushed and did not know what to do. On the drive home mulled over how to tell Samantha that I had lost my job. I knew the situation would be instant fuel to start an argument, so I decided against telling her. Every day I left home as if I was going to work. Meanwhile, I continued searching for a job, without success. When weeks passed and I never offered money for the baby, Samantha guessed that I was not working.

On April 15, 1999 I had my third episode after a heated argument with Samantha and she called the police. At this point it seemed like Samantha called the police every time I came to the house. I was transported to Eastern State Hospital in Williamsburg, VA, where after processing I was taken to the mental ward.

Waking up in a psyche cell was not something that I planned for in my life. So it was very hard for me to fathom that I was mentally ill and I never accepted the state doctor's diagnosis. As a result, I pressed my way into my faith, knowing that GOD was the only being who could rescue me from this black hole into which I was fast spiraling down. I did, nonetheless, accept this new situation as another obstacle that I was going to overcome -- by any means necessary.

Initially, I chose not to interact with anyone on the mental ward floor, because I knew that I did not belong there and I certainly was not mentally ill or crazy. When the nurses made their rounds to give out medication, I always refused to take it. I was trying to figure out what the hell was wrong with me. Nobody in my family that I knew of had ever been in a mental hospital. I had been stripped of all the material things of the world and everything I loved and cared for. Once again I felt like I was being abandoned by the world. What I did participate in was the church services every Sunday morning. There were great deals of Jesus want to be are in the audience, so the services were sometimes hard to get through because of all the unwanted outbursts. To be overly religious or to preach the word in a state hospital was sometimes not a good idea. The walking prophet act was always interpreted the wrong way by the mental ward staff and your medication levels went up -- instantaneously.

There were people from every socioeconomic level on my floor. Lawyers, Muslims, Christians, businessmen, academicians and other voluntarily admitted themselves. I just kept telling myself that this was a minor setback and I must not bend or let my spirit be broken while I was in the hospital. Getting back on my feet was the easy, but being healed of the mental illness demon I left in the hands of my Savior. I prayed many times during the day every day, and would cry myself to sleep most nights. I was consumed by the thought that I was being punished for something I did or did not do for GOD. Sometimes I wondered about the end times: When Jesus comes back to this world under cover might He be taken away and labeled crazy?

Some of our most talented and intelligent people in the present day and throughout the history of the world dealt with issues of mental illness. People of the world please do not be so quick to call someone crazy just because you do not understand them.

May 2, 1999 it was my 27th birthday and I had to spend it in a state mental hospital = around outcasts, with crazy labels attached to them. Many mentally ill people simple do not have the resources or support from their families to help in the fight to live a normal life. Some patients were admitted to the hospital indefinitely, and were housed in a separate building from the newly admitted mentally ill patients. The groups of buildings were reminiscent of dorms on a college campus. There are many activities set up for all patients, such as dances, bingo night, holiday and social events as if they were in a normal community.

The day of my birthday was also an opportunity for the mental ward staff to escort me to visit my care team doctor, a meeting which they had previously attempted to schedule, without success. It had been noticed that I was somewhat in a good mood and mingling in with other patients on the floor. A female orderly approached me and asked if I would be interested in going to see my care team today. I responded with a big Kool-Ade smile, yes, because I refused to let anything spoil my B-Day. As I was escorted from the B-Ward floor and around the nurses' station I inhaled the fresh air. You see, it was often quite stuffy on the B-Ward floor, since for security purposes all of the windows were closed and locked. Upon reaching the meeting room door I got a little nervous because having never been in a mental hospital before I had no idea what to expect.

LIVING 2 DIE OR DYING 2 LIVE

Moving around the big conference size table I sat in the only chair that was not occupied. My entire care team was there, which consisted of my psychiatrist, psychologist, social worker, nurse, and a few other people who were obtaining information for a study on mental illnesses. The meeting with my doctor did not last long, because I started to feel threatened by the words that were issuing from his mouth. And at that point I did not want to accept or believe what he was telling me when such words as Manic Depressive, Bi-Polar, Homicidal Manic, and walking time bomb, kept ringing in my head.

Once I shook off being called all these names, I told the doctor he was a quack and fucking crazy, and he could shove the diagnosis and medicine up his ass. Everyone in the room just froze and went into panic mode. Here was this big black man screaming at this scrawny little white doctor, who would have gotten his wig split, if I could have jumped across that big ass conference table. As the hospital security team rushed into the meeting room and immediately subdued me, I was escorted by security back to my ward floor. I was then ordered by the nurse in charge to be put in one of the solitary rooms until I calmed down. Approximately 10 minutes after being confined, the mental ward nurse came in with the male staff and asked me to turn around and drop my pants. The nurse hit me with a double dose of what the patients on the wards called liquid kryptonite in each butt cheek. One dose could slow down an elephant, and two doses could put a patient to sleep for a couple of days.

On a different day in my ward a patient received a double dose of the liquid kryptonite that he did not take well. When other patients, me included me, did not see the patient for a couple of days, we thought the nurse had given him too much kryptonite and killed him. The patient never came out of his room; he missed his meals and patients on the mental ward floor do not miss meals no matter what their situation, unless they are really too sick or ill. Sometimes when meals were served a couple of the patients and I would play a trick by telling the other patients who were truly insane that their food was tainted or that it had been laced with poison by the staff. The patients got scared and refused to eat, gladly giving us their meals.

After a month in Eastern State Hospital I was released and caught a flight back to Austin, Texas to my parent's house. I was still nowhere near functional when I arrived in Austin at the airport and the medication that I was taking made me dizzy and light headed. I was reluctant at first to take the medicine that I was prescribed, because I really thought that the type of medicine I was on would do more harm than good to my mind and body.

It was ironic for me to come back to my mother's house, inasmuch as it was something that I said I would never do, but GOD brings you back to a situation for a reason. In order to get past a negative moment in life, one must first accept what happened, at which time that bad experience becomes easier to handle. I was even more screwed up in the mind when I left Eastern State hospital, but was very happy to have been released. When I did take the medicine that was prescribed, I would stay in the bed and only get up when it was time to eat and go back to sleep. Do you see the trend here? There were times that I did not know if it was morning or night, not to mention what day it was.

GOD had brought me back to my mother and step-dad's house to confront why they had been against me as a child and chose to abandon me altogether. GOD does not make mistakes and being in my situation, I was not able to work or take care of myself and my parents were forced to be my primary care givers. I knew GOD was there with me every day, because I stayed on my knee's praying everyday for two years. The short time that I was awake I took advantage of the time and read my mom's Bible. By now my mother and stepfather were born again Christians and living for GOD, "Glory Hallelujah." All the many prayers that I had prayed as a child were at last being answered. Thank You GOD!

On the negative side, my weight went from an in-shape 220 pounds to an obese 340 pounds during the two-years that I resided with my parents. Reading the word of GOD kept me focused. It lit my light of hope and my renewed my trust that GOD would pull me through this dark tunnel and prove the Eastern State Hospital doctors wrong.

I had become a person who was unable to take care of himself; I needed my family's help. On the other hand, I did not want to be a burden on my parents, because I knew that they were just barely making ends met with the money that they had coming in. But, without question this was a test from GOD to see how my parents would treat the new challenge that He had brought to their doorstep. I had unknowingly and officially become the black sheep of my entire family, because my condition is taboo in the black community. Mental Illness is not regularly and openly discussed among African-Americans.

I chose to sleep in the backroom of my parent's trailer; I stayed in my room most of the time, preferring to have minimal contact with my parents and other relatives who came to visit from time to time. During the six months I stayed with my parents I probably ventured outside once or twice. I had totally lost interest in the things that I once enjoyed -- the little things that we sometimes take for granted like watching a football or basketball game on T.V., or just hanging out socializing with friends. I felt that I was damaged goods and knew that starting and maintaining relationships with females was out of the question. Even though my young daughter (baby girl) was too young to talk on the phone, just hearing her making baby sounds was more than enough for me. Baby girl was the only person who loved me unconditionally and did not see any faults when she stared at me with her light brown eyes. I tried to call her everyday so that she would not forget daddy's voice until I was able to see her again. I knew I had to reclaim my life and overcome this illness, so as I prayed every night to my Lord and Savior I asked that he heal my mind and body. I knew that as baby girl grew into a child, young teen, young adult, and woman she was going to need her daddy. As I started to come around and to gradually interact with my family, my mom and step-dad initiated discussions about different verses in the bible. We were having informal bible study in the living room of the house, which lead me to hunger for more of GOD's word.

My mother, who still did not really comprehend what I was going through, took me shopping for new clothes one Saturday afternoon. She planned to take me to church the next day and knew that I would say that I did not have anything to wear due to my huge weight gain and low self-esteem because of it. It was a joy getting out of the house and shopping for new clothes. My mom kept telling me that I was somebody and she wanted me to start believing in myself and caring about my appearance. I had let myself go at this point; my hair had grown into an afro; my facial hair was now a beard; and my fingernails were as long as a woman's. After the clothes shopping I went and got a haircut and cleaned myself up like I did the illness. It was nice of my mom to do this for me. I had heard years ago that a mother is always in their child's corner through good and bad times. A Mother believes in their child when the world has written you off.

The next day was Sunday morning and my mother woke me up early and told me to talk a bath, iron my clothes, and get dressed for church. The new clothes she had bought for me alleviated any of my prior excuses to avoid going to church; I was just nervous about the people with whom I went to high school or the people that I knew in the town seeing me as this overweight person. I was ashamed of myself for gaining all the weight and contracting the mysterious mental condition. As I attempted to drag myself out of the bed I still felt drunk from the medication that was supposed to help me regain a functional life. I lay awake on my bed at which time the devil's voice advised me not to get out of bed and to just lie back down. Because the devil knew that I was going to church to worship GOD, he tried to convince me that nobody at the church could help me. Where my mother was taking me, I would remain a lost soul, he said. I replied to the Devil, telling him, "Loose Devil! I bind you in the mighty name of Jesus." After my rebuke the Devil's voice started to fade away. When I finished getting dressed I grabbed my mother's Bible and informed my parents that I would be waiting in the car.

I still remember the drive to Arise Ministries; my mother had visited the church and worshipped there several times before and received a strong prophetic word. I was in and out of consciousness while I sat in the backseat of the car and could barely keep my eyes open. This was the first time that I stayed awake this long; and the car ride started to feel more like an speeding ambulance which was rushing me to the hospital. But this ride was even better, because the emergency was for the purpose of saving my soul. I was being rushed to GOD's hospital. GOD's anointed personnel would be waiting to lift me up so that GOD could perform spiritual surgery on me.

When my parents and I finally reached Arise Ministries we sat in the car for a little while and just prayed to GOD, asking Him to heal me and open a door for me. Entering Arise Ministries I knew that my mother had led me to the right place, as I could feel GOD's presence everywhere. The Arise members warmly greeted us and escorted us to our seats. Once, we were seated I noticed that this church was diverse -- every nationality was represented Apostle Russell Vance was preaching the word of GOD and half way through - the service he noticed me. -GOD had shown him my spirit and immediately I was called to the altar. Apostle Vance then told me that he did not have the answers to my many questions, but what he did have was the word of GOD. He advised me -to - lean- on and trusts GOD -for my healing. So as I returned to my seat my light of hope got a little brighter. I appreciated those words that the Apostle had spoken into my life. GOD was just confirming my prayers through Apostle Vance and showed me that the Apostle was a true man of GOD. During this time in Austin, Texas there seemed to be a dark cloud over the city for believers in GOD's word, because so many money hungry false prophets from out of state had set up shop in Austin to drain GOD's people of all their monetary possessions. These false prophets would only give you spiritual guidance if your tithe was the right amount, which was whatever the false prophet- requested when they said a prayer for you. There was the 1,000-dollar line, 500-dollar line, 250-dollar line, 100 dollar line, and whatever you had line to hear what GOD had told them to tell you. When the money started to get really good they would - bring - other false prophets - to town to give their GOD sent message a big event.

These spiritual shenanigans caused a spiritual black cloud to form over the city of Austin. I always wondered why these prophets were not performing the so-called miracles in their own hometowns. The praying miracle scheme worked for a while until GOD's believers caught onto what they were doing and stopped attending their services. The prophets tried to elevate their praying miracle scheme by continuing to hold these - "special services" in hotels around the city. Once the hotels began demanding payment for the use of their conference rooms the false prophets decided to move to another hotel in the city. When the hotels did not receive payment for the outstanding invoices for - rental of the conference rooms, the hotels - informed the police-. Several -of the top false prophets escaped the police raids at the hotels. However, the false prophets - on the low-end of the totem pole were arrested and sentenced to prison.

When people are taken advantage of in the name of GOD there is no need to worry. You must - remain focused on GOD and every-thing will work out in your favor. These mischievous "prophets" will not have to answer to anyone on - earth, but when the day comes for them to stand in front of the Lord.

"Glory Hallelujah." They will reap what they sowed.

As the months passed by and I continued to visit Arise Ministries off and on, I received positive and spiritual words of encouragement which fed my spirit. Slowly I began - to feel better - with each passing day. Ultimately, I was well enough to leave the house on warm and sunny days, rather than keeping to the bed and sleeping away my life-. Soon I had - productive days and was able to take care of myself. I then started to look for an apartment and when I found an apartment that I liked, I moved out of my parent's house.

I also attended mental health sessions at the Veterans

Hospital, which appointments - were scheduled 3 to 6 months apart. There was a new doctor at each appointment. The services that I received impressed me that the doctors l were practicing on me with various medicines to treat mental illness. This was my feeling, since during each appointment the doctors would write a new prescription apparently to see what would be the affect. Being treated as though I were a willing member of a clinical trial was most undesirable. Consequently, I took the road to recovery from mental illness into my own hands.

The diagnosis given at the state hospital in Virginia stuck with me for a while, even though there were never any tests to confirm such diagnosis. Likewise, no tests were conducted to determine if I was suffering from a different mental illness. Therefore, I continued to question whether I was in fact Bi-Polar, considering there are no present day links to Bi-polar disorder caused by military service. The doctors informed me that I was suffering from Bi-polar because my family had a history of the condition. This was when I knew and the doctors confirmed that they did not have a clue as to what was going on with me. It was easy and probably politically mandatory for the VA Hospital doctors to write me off as Bi-polar than to give me the proper diagnosis of Post Traumatic Stress Disorder (PTSD).

Not really knowing what Bi-polar was and how someone contracted it compelled me to join a Bi-polar support group in the community. Such action provided an opportunity to become educated about the illness and also to meet people who had it. At the first meeting I had nothing to contribute to the discussion and was more like a fly on the wall. I simply surveyed the group members to glean information about their illness as well as what treatments they were using to combat it. Attending the meetings taught me that I did not have the same symptoms the

LIVING 2 DIE OR DYING 2 LIVE

Bi-polar group members were experiencing, nor did I do the things that were being revealed. I did receive fruitful information and useful knowledge of what medications were the most effective for treating some of their symptoms. Additionally, it became clear which medications were ineffective.

The support group acted more like family, and trusted each other enough to keep confidential whatever was discussed in the meetings. Group members also gave positive and helpful advice to those in the group who were in crisis. Wrestling with a mental illness on a daily basis is a challenge by itself and there are no overnight cures. That is why I patiently and methodically found solutions to my recovery one day at a time. With GODS help I remained hopeful and positive. Some people in the support group were very functional with the right mix of medications and held down fulltime jobs. Hearing their stories made my light of hope get a little brighter and my recovery the more attainable.

My relationship with Samantha eventually ended; I guess my illness was too much for her to handle. I continued to have a strong relationship with my daughters even though they lived in Virginia and I had moved back to Austin, Texas.

By September 2002 I accepted that Samantha and I would not become a family again, and she told me that she wanted to move on. We agreed to split and I then started to focus more on myself and to be the best dad for my baby girl.

I enrolled in online classes at St. Leo University and got my college credits transferred from Hampton University. After evaluation of my transcripts the online counselor at St. Leo University informed me that I only needed a few more classes to complete my bachelor's degree. Because of the volume of classes offered by the online program, and the shorter semesters than on actual university campuses, I would finish my online program in accounting at St. Leo University within the year. Fortunately, I had somewhat of a grip on my malady and was able to concentrate and shake off most of its effects.

My classes through Saint Leo University on-line program was paid for by the Vocational Rehabilitation Program of the Veterans Administration. I then went to the local Veterans hospital and signed up for vocational rehab, as I was still somewhat out on a limb and could not stay awake in my voc rehab counselor's office.

Taking classes online worked out great for me, because I could finish my degree without any physical interaction with people. I did not want to be around anybody - friends or family and therefore refused to attend family outings.

11

Using God as a Guiding Light

September 2003, I took the final online course at St. Leo University and graduated with a B.A. in accounting. At last, I had received my college degree, fulfilling one of my childhood dreams. I remember as a little boy praying to GOD to give me the wisdom and knowledge to achieve and obtain a college degree. This was a huge accomplishment for me and I felt that I was moving in the right direction.

The rejoicing ended when I was unable to find a fulltime accounting job. It seemed like I applied to every single accounting position in the country and not one company gave me the chance to prove my skills, knowledge and ability. This created a great deal of stress in my life because I had my baby girl to support and I wanted to give her the world. Some of the stress was relieved when I rethought my situation and decided that the time was perfect to start my own consulting business. I always dreamed of being my own boss and working for myself. The opportunity to do so happened sooner than I had anticipated. Since I was a little boy, I had been a business visionary, and some of my hopes were about to be realized.

USING GOD AS A GUIDING LIGHT

The holidays were quickly approaching, so I decided to get a retail job at the local mall until one of the accounting jobs came through for me, or I attained my first consulting contract. The retail job at the local mall was a fulltime position, which allowed me to interact with customers for free and to selectively pass out my business cards to customers who requested my accounting services. I was not your average retail salesman. I analyzed every situation, and found ways to benefit from each one. The retail store was a great place to network, because I chose to work in the men's dress shirt section. Most of my customers were females looking for dress shirts for their dad, husband, brother, boyfriend, and special friends. I was also able to give my personal styling tips and advice about men to these women, while getting my Mack Daddy game back on track. To some customers who came to my section of the store, I acted as counselor and confidant. They told me their personal stories and the happenings in their lives. I was always a good listener, and when asked gave them my honest assessment of their situation. The majority of my advice was given to women in relationships with cheating boyfriends. I confided that if a man's stomach is kept full and his sexuality exhausted, most men do not think about or have the energy to cheat. The first mistake women make while in a relationship is to cut out the bedroom activities. This is tantamount to telling their boyfriend IT'S OKAY to CHEAT.

I enjoyed going to work because in the retail business each day becomes a different and new adventure. I began to feel so good about myself that I stopped taking my daily medication. The daily medication that I was prescribed took away my creative and entrepreneurial spirit, replacing them with fatigue and antisocial behavior. As I ceased taking the medication, my grip on reality began to slip away. One-day I decide not to take any of my prescribed medication, as I -- or the devil -- had convinced me that I did not need any more medication.

12

Phoenix

All hell broke loose on a cold day in the middle of the month in December 2003. Suddenly I started to hear voices ordering me to perform a strategically military style road march to the nearest bus stop in my neighborhood. My instantaneous change of actions should have made the losing touch with reality meter spike. Why did it not occur to me that I did not have to walk anywhere since my Ford Expedition (Eddie Bauer) stood in the parking lot of my apartment complex? Nonetheless, I got dressed for the cold weather march and marched to the bus stop that was less than a half of a mile from my apartment. On reaching the city bus stop I saw a guy that I knew from my childhood. We greeted each other and then proceeded to talk about the things that we did in our youth. I was trying very hard to maintain a normal conversation with this person until the city bus arrived. Finally I noticed the bus coming down the street and politely ended the conversation. As the bus came to a complete stop and the doors opened, I then stepped aboard paid my fare, made a bee line to the back, and sat in the last seat on the right. This seat provided a window view, which allowed me to watch the ever changing landscape of the city and the speeding cars that passed by. Abruptly, a voice told me to get off the bus. So, I pulled the cord for the bus to stop at the next stop, as the city bus slowed down and came to a complete stop I exited in a location two miles from my job in the mall. During the road march to my job I also told myself I do not need my job anymore because I was going to start training to either go back into the Army or play in the NFL. This was when the second flag should have gone up, because the last time I was able to play any sport was in May 1993, when I was deployed with 567th TC went on a training mission to Roosevelt Roads, Puerto Rico where I injured my knee by tearing my Anterior Crucicet Ligament (ACL).

When I arrived at the retail store, I was greeted by my fellow employees. I headed straight to my managers office, where I had left a package of Polo dress socks that I had purchased a day before. When I asked my manager for my socks, he asked me for a receipt. That's when I went into defense mode, and began yelling at the manger to give me my socks that I had paid for. I told him that I did not have the f----- receipt. Thereafter, I made a big spectacle in front of the other employees about the manager not trusting that I had purchased the socks.

Marching to the men's shoe department, I asked for the most expensive pair of dress shoes available, and ordered the shoe salesman to put it on my manager's tab. Security was alerted and when they arrived we argued for a brief moment, after which my manager gave me the package of polo socks and I was escorted out of the store.

Back in my apartment I lay down until the late afternoon, and awoke to a voice telling me to get out of bed. I did and by this time my mother was knocking on my front door. She had come by to check on me, and on seeing that I was acting weird called the police. The police came but did not take me to jail because I had not committed a crime and was in my own apartment.

Mother pleaded with me to get some help, but I refused and told her that nothing was wrong with me and she could not control me anymore. She stayed with me a couple of hours after the police left and until I had calmed down. Later that night I watched the classic movie *Scarface* as I often did. However, I refused to watch the ending of the movie because I believed if I were Scarface I would have left the drug game on top.

At 1:00 o'clock in the morning I looked out of one of my bedroom windows while seated in a chair. It was then that I decided to make a statement to the entire apartment complex that I was nobody to mess with. So I started throwing my furniture off my second floor balcony, first my dining table chairs, then all of my clothes, suits, then all of my DVD movies and VHS cassette tapes, and the grand finale was my 42"inch television. As the television hit the side of the sidewalk, the crashing sound woke up the rest of the apartment complex. I was screaming at the top of my lungs at law enforcement as they sped onto the scene. The police officers saw all of the furniture broken on the ground from its flight from the second floor balcony and asked me why I threw my furniture out. I informed the cops that I was doing a little spring-cleaning and would be getting brand new furniture. Then I told them that they could look through the rubble and take anything they wanted. There were some people outside now that had formed a small crowd and was looking at me from the ground. I invited the crowd to my apartment and told them that they could have anything in my apartment. The police officers, who had determined that I was either high on drugs or had some mental issues, tried to get me to come downstairs and talk to them, but I refused, telling them what I thought about the police force. To this day I still do not know why I took off all of my clothes and threw them at the police officers.

When started to make my way back inside my apartment from the balcony that was attached to my front door that over looked the front parking lot. I could hear the police officers boots running up the stairs to my apartment. Once the police officers had me on the ground and handcuffed, they placed me in a squad car and tied my feet together with rope.

I was transported to Austin State Hospital where I was released to the staff for evaluation and then led to the mental ward. Once at the mental ward I had totally lost my grip on reality; I thought the staff was going to kill me. So I ran from the staff, but they tackled me to the floor and dragged me away to a solitary room, where I spent the night, unaware that the door was never locked and I could have left by simply pushing it open.

During the night I kept hearing voices, but I tried blocking them out telling the voices to go away. Once morning came I was introduced to my treatment team. A nurse at the hospital who took a special interest in me had taped to one of the windows a butterfly that I had drawn for her. Seeing the butterfly on the glass window really lifted my spirits.

With each passing day on the mental ward I improved, but still was not well enough to reenter society. At Austin State Hospital all patients had to attend classes after breakfast. While the patients were in the dining hall t all room doors were locked. So when patients returned from breakfast they could not retire to their rooms for the rest of the day. Patients' involvement in the structured classes allowed them to earn points to be used for gifts or special privileges. These earned points were then given to the staff to be honored when patients redeemed the points

PHOENIX

for weekend passes, making a phone call after normal patient phone time was over. After a couple of weeks had passed by I still was not well enough to leave so I demanded that I be sent to the Veterans Hospital in Waco, Texas.

13

Pray 4 ME

I was transported to the Waco Veterans Hospital in the middle of the night, and checked into the mental ward at around 2:00 a.m. The veterans' hospital staff seemed to be more relaxed than the staff at the state hospital in Austin. The nurse that checked my vital signs noticed that my body temperature was a little high. I told her that I had not been feeling well for the past couple of days. I had caught my first cold of the flu season and the fever made me sweat as if I had been working out.

Being sent to the Waco VA from the Austin State Hospital was like night and day as far as the treatment for my misdiagnosed mental illness. Most state and private hospitals do not want to treat veterans with mental illness because the administration feels that vet patients are too much of a threat to staff and other patients. During my stay at the Veterans hospital my treatment team knew exactly what was wrong with me and started treating me for posttraumatic stress disorder (PTSD). Once I started taking the right medicine for my unexplained behavior and psychotic thoughts I immediately started to function as a normal person. It was as though I had awakened from a never-ending nightmare. After years in the state system during which I took a great deal of medication that kept me in bed, only waking up to eat my meals was just putting a blanket over my illness. My mind and body felt like I was getting high everyday and not relieving the symptoms and feelings that I was experiencing and explaining to the doctors. I just stayed on my knees night and day asking GOD to bring me out of this black hole that I seemed to have fallen into. I repented for my sins and I knew I was reaping the sins of being a liar, womanizer, committing adultery, and living a life that had the potential to earn me a first class ticket to hell.

Back home in Austin from the Waco VA, I followed up with my appointments at the Austin VA hospital. The doctor at the Austin VA did not think that I had PTSD, and therefore I was required to take a PTSD test given by a PTSD specialist. If a veteran did not pass this test it was concluded that the veteran did not have PTSD. I failed the test -- probably like many other veterans -- and was denied benefits. I guess the hospital was trying to save the government money by disallowing the PTSD diagnosis.

There were times at the VA hospital that seemed unreal to me -- the things I had to go through just to receive the proper treatment for my military service-connected illness. The government quickly forgets that upon entering the military to serve their country these young men and women are in the best shape of their lives. If recruits were not in the best shape or not able to serve their country, the recruits would not pass the mandatory entry physical exam that supposedly helps weed out non-fit recruits.

On January 31, 2004 I was released from the Waco Veterans Hospital after a 30-day "vacation". When I finally got back into my apartment after the long drive from Waco, I prayed to GOD to give me the strength to overcome my situation and remove all of the demons I had allowed into my mind and body because of my lifestyle, and disobedience to His word. I then promised myself that I would never go back to any mental hospital. And yet to avoid returning to any mental hospital I had to always take the medicine that the doctor had prescribed for me. Now that I was on the right medication and the VA had at last properly diagnosis me with PTSD, I was able to take control of my life, because my daughters needed me and I could not help them if I were constantly in and out of mental health facilities. I knew I had to step up my game and be the man that GOD had destined me to be.

My daughters gave me the motivation needed to make lemons into lemonade. So, I faithfully read my Bible and prayed to my Heavenly Father every night and visited different churches in Austin. I was now waiting on GOD to send me a sign or lead me to the church with which he wanted me to make a covenant.

During this time I reevaluated my job situation and decided that I needed to go back to school and get a master's degree in business. I have always had an entrepreneurial spirit, but wanted to have a backup plan if my vision was never realized. A master's degree would give me the training and guidance needed to be an effective manager for some company and more marketable to employers.

I enrolled in graduate courses at a local university, but had a gut feeling that this university was not where GOD wanted me to be. I had earned a bachelor's degree, but was still unable to find a fulltime government job. Doors around me were slamming shut, which angered me at times. Where had all the dedication and time spent getting a college degree gotten me? It was beginning to appear as though the degree was worthless.

PRAY 4 ME

The only job that did call me back was a federal job doing taxes, but it only lasted for the tax season. Then the road to my MBA degree got even rockier, as after three semesters taking graduate courses I was dismissed from the University for making "Cs" in two of my classes. I refused to get upset or worry because I knew that GOD was with me. I had been praying about the way I was being treated in some of my classes by some of the professors. So instead of being angry I just rejoiced in and praised GODs name. Then GOD opened a door for me, and before I got my official dismissal letter from the local university I was accepted into another MBA program at a different university.

February 1, 2006 I was officially accepted to the University of Phoenix and most of my graduate courses from my previous school transferred, which would allow me to receive an MBA by the end of the year. Never let anyone tell you, you cannot do something because GOD will always make that person a LIAR. I was like a phoenix raising from the ashes and truly believe that GOD took me out of the fire and allowed me to rise above all obstacles. My life seemed to get a great deal easier when I let go and let GOD take control. I felt for the first time in my life that all the pressures of the world had been lifted off of my shoulders.

July 12, 2006, 6:00 a.m. I received a call from my mother telling me that my granddad had called and told her that he needed help on the breeding horse ranch where he had worked for 30+ years. The owner had rented out some horse stalls to horse owners who were having a horse show on her ranch for the next two days. I told my mom that I was on my way and to tell my granddad not to worry. When I arrived I had never seen my granddad so frustrated about anything. Up until this point my granddad never had to depend on anybody; he always took care of all his problems by himself. He was born around 1930

-- give or takes a few years. I say this is because he told me that he changed his birth date, so that he would be old enough to get a driver's license. Once my granddad stopped thanking me for showing up, I told him that's what family is for. See how GOD works?

I continued to work with my granddad after the horse show was over and enjoyed every story he told me about his youth. Even though he told the same stories over and over again, I listened as if it was the first time I had heard them.

My granddad grew up around horses. When he was about eleven years of age he was not tall enough to mount a horse, so he put the horse in a ditch and jumped on the horse bareback and had been riding horses ever since. He advised me to be a gentlemen towards women and to always be a man of my word, because your word is all you have and once that is tarnished then you are left with nothing. This was a man that worked in construction as a youth and helps build most of the buildings around the city of Austin. Granddad's favorite story was when he had to transport a trailer full of horses from Houston to Austin. He would get into detail how he would navigate the 18-wheeler on the curves and turns with precision. He felt the truck drivers today do not know how to drive. Granddad and I laughed uproariously when he would see 18-wheeler trucks and trailers jack knife on u-turns while I drove him to his doctor's appointment. I sit back now and cherish every moment I was able to spend with my granddad, because he passed away a few months later. "I LOVE YOU PA PA."

Who would have thought with my experience and education that I would be shoveling horse manure everyday on a horse ranch? Sometimes you have to not look at what you are doing in the present with a secular eye. You have to ask yourself, why GOD has me in this situation and what I can learn from

PRAY 4 ME

it. GOD never makes mistakes. You have to also ask yourself am I doing GOD's will or the will of man. At first I questioned why GOD had brought me to the horse ranch. Now I know why. GOD had brought me to the ranch to spend time with a man whose name I had borne my entire life to bring us closer together. And even more than our closeness, this was a wise man from whose wisdom I could gain immeasurable benefits. Furthermore, this would be the last time I saw my granddad and was my final opportunity to learn some life lessons and knowledge from a man who was not educated in the traditional way. GOD knew what I needed from my granddad before I left Austin, Texas and moved to Atlanta, Georgia. My days working at the horse ranch with my granddad were only set up by the good GOD that I serve.

I was a couple of months from graduating with my MBA. Praise the LORD, after which I planned to pack up my car and move to Atlanta (The New Black Hollywood) to start a new chapter in my life. I wish I could have taken my granddad with me.

In November 2006 I graduated from the University of Phoenix's MBA program and moved to Atlanta, Georgia. Where, I currently have lived for the past two years. Atlanta has slowed down a great deal since the Freaknik days in the early 90's and has become a city of powerful and rich blacks. Black Hollywood aka Atlanta has shown me that it is possible for blacks to support each other and still remain positive. Making excuses why you cannot pick up the cross is easy to do, but just remember that GOD gives you wisdom and knowledge to make your own lifestyle choices. Many believe that GOD will always forgive them for their sinful lives, because they repent every day. This is true as long as you have time on this earth and breathe in your body. Because, when your internal clock goes off and you die and you are standing in front of GOD for your judgment, you cannot tell GOD that you were not ready and that you need more time. Sin is sin and righteousness is to follow God; these two paths cannot be walked at the same time. Walk with Christ and you will have eternal life, but when you walk with the devil you will be destroyed and cast into the lake of fire to burn forever. Living a Christian life has brought me the happiness and love I so desired my entire life. Christ continues to guide my steps every day on a path of righteousness. I pray that my name appears in the book of life, when the Lord comes back for his people.

Atlanta is the place I call home, because I know that this is the place GOD has prepared for me. I just wish that I would have let GOD take control of my life a great deal earlier.

To My Readers

Time is precious -- never take it for granted, because you cannot rewind or fast forward time. Only GOD knows the beginning and the end. So while you still have time, get your life together. Do it now, because tomorrow may be too late! Live the life your Heavenly Father has already planned for you. When your time is up in this world and you close your eyes for the last time, there should be no regrets. You cannot ask for more time to do the things you did not have time to do, like dreams that were never followed, and people you did not get a chance to say I LOVE YOU to. Let your past be just that and your present a prosperous life. I would like to take this time to say thank you for taking the time to read my testimony. I cannot end this book without a passage from the bible.

This Bible verse comes from the New Living Translation Bible in the book of

Matthew 24:4-14. GOD BLESSES YOU!!!

"Don't let anyone mislead you, for many will come in my name, claiming,' I am the Messiah'. They will deceive many, and you will hear of wars and threats of wars, but don't panic. Yes, these things must take place, but the end won't follow immediately.

Nations will go to war against nations, and Kingdom against Kingdom. There will be famines and earthquakes in many parts of the world. But all this is only the first of birth pains, with more to come.

"Then you will be arrested, persecuted, and killed. You will be hated all over the world because you are my followers. And many will turn away from me and betray and hate each other. And many false prophets will appear and will deceive many people. Sin will be rampant everywhere and the love of many will grow cold.

But the ones who endure to the end will be saved. And the Good News about the Kingdom will be preached throughout the whole world, so that all nations will hear it; and then the end will come.

So let me ask you this question, are you

LIVING 2 DIE OR DYING 2 LIVE"

Contact Information:

Barron K. Haywood, MBA

barron.k.haywoodmba@gmail.com

Facebook: Barron K Haywood Mba

Thanks for the support

CPSIA information can be obtained
at www.ICGtesting.com
Printed in the USA
BVHW080603180122
626472BV00001B/50